HARRY
STYLES

HARRY STYLES

Every Piece of Me

Louisa Jepson

**SIMON &
SCHUSTER**

London · New York · Sydney · Toronto · New Delhi

A CBS COMPANY

First published in Great Britain by Simon & Schuster UK Ltd, 2013
A CBS COMPANY

1 3 5 7 9 10 8 6 4 2

Simon & Schuster UK Ltd
1st Floor
222 Gray's Inn Road
London WC1X 8HB

www.simonandschuster.co.uk

Simon & Schuster Australia, Sydney
Simon & Schuster India, New Delhi

A CIP catalogue record for this book
is available from the British Library

Hardback ISBN: 978-1-47112-847-9
Trade Paperback ISBN: 978-1-47112-858-5
Ebook ISBN: 978-1-47112-849-3

Printed

PROLOGUE

'Last night was the best thing I have ever done'

As the lights dimmed, the noise was deafening. Ear-splitting screams cut through the crisp evening air and could be heard for miles around New York City.

A staggering 20,000 fans had turned out to see Harry Styles and the rest of One Direction in the flesh at the fabled Madison Square Garden, the Big Apple's most iconic music venue. It was the hottest ticket in town and many teenage fans had fallen to the ground in uncontrollable hysterics after getting their hands on one.

Flags from every corner of the globe waved high in the crowd, showing their support. Girls craned their necks to try to get a better view and camera bulbs flashed endlessly as the fans tried to see if the boys were already on the stage.

Rows of burly, expressionless security guards lined the platform, which was fitted with a huge runway, so the quintet could serenade the fans from all sides.

Harry and the boys had managed to sell out the arena, the third biggest in the world, in the record time of less than one minute, so they were under huge pressure to deliver. The nerves backstage were palpable, with Harry tweeting 'nervous' to his 9 million followers on the social networking site. All the band members had struggled to sleep the night before because they were so high on adrenaline.

Earlier that day Harry had posted a message to his fans reading: 'Thinking about what we were doing three years ago today . . . Today we play Madison Square Garden. We can never thank you enough. We love you. xx'

In the crowd his proud mum Anne Cox, dad Des Styles and stepdad Robin Twist watched on. After a whirlwind romance, his new girlfriend, pretty US pop star Taylor Swift, was in the wings too, waiting to celebrate at the lavish private after-party. Also along for the ride were Liam Payne, Zayn Malik, Louis Tomlinson and Niall Horan's nearest and dearest. It was the largest gathering of 1D's families and friends since the final of *The X Factor* in December 2010.

The minutes ticked by: at last, the historic moment had arrived. The immense stage lit up in an explosion of blue and white and the 1D logo illuminated the backdrop. The crowd continued to roar, making a thunderous noise, and glowing images of the band played in a moving montage.

Then, as a countdown went from ten to one, cannons

threw out great clouds of smoke high into the air and the crowd were on their feet, bellowing as loudly as they possibly could in anticipation.

The blue spotlights bore down on Harry, Zayn, Niall, Louis and Liam as they burst into a rendition of their uptempo hit, 'Up All Night', from the front of the runway. They were all pumped up, their hearts hammering and their ears ringing from the noise of the crowd. Harry bounced up and down on the far side of the stage with an infectious grin and cheeky hip thrusts, and egged the audience on to dance with him. Many fans almost had cardiac arrests as Harry gave them a smouldering stare or steely gaze. By the time the boys had finished the first song, a pair of knickers had been thrown at him – the first of a few pairs – a bra and an iPhone would follow as the evening unfolded.

They whipped the crowd into a frenzy with a medley of hits, including 'Na Na Na', 'Stand Up', 'I Wish', 'Gotta Be You' and 'More Than This' and Harry, overwhelmed by the moment, commented: 'This place is bloody huge,' to roaring applause.

They then launched into a cover version of Wheatus' 'Teenage Dirtbag', complete with pyrotechnics, before performing 'Live While We're Young', 'Tell Me A Lie' and 'Everything About You'.

In the middle of the show, the five-piece answered some questions from Twitter, such as 'Who has the loudest section?' – cue lots and lots of screams – 'Who can jump the highest?' (Niall because Harry's jeans were too tight) and 'If you were an animal what would you be and what would your mating call be?' Harry had fans bent double with laughter when he said his mating call would be to introduce himself and say, 'Hello, I'm the Real Liam Payne. Nice to meet you.' Other tweets asked them to impersonate New York cab drivers and wondered what they would do if a chicken attacked them.

Then they sang 'Moments', 'I Want' and 'Save You Tonight', when they threw themselves into the delighted crowd and had photos taken with fans, while the nervous security guards manhandled them away from some of the more eager followers who were grabbing their clothes.

Next, during the performance of their latest acoustic ballad, 'Little Things', they were joined on stage by their good pal Ed Sheeran, who had written the track. He was stunned by the rapturous reception. They concluded the set with 'One Thing', 'Kiss You' and 'C'mon C'mon' and, for an encore, they bounded back on stage for the immensely popular anthem, 'What Makes You Beautiful'. Harry had a bra hurled at him and ran around with it onstage before throwing it up into the air with a laugh. The whole crowd were singing along in unison: teenagers and parents; young and old; British and American.

Niall told the screaming audience: 'This is the best night of our lives. You guys have travelled from all around the world and we cannot believe what has happened here tonight. Thank you so much.'

The group had a big hug, while confetti and giant balloons flew around the arena, and as the gig ended Harry declared: 'I have never been so proud.'

The gig, their last full-length one for 2012, was the most incredible way to cap off a truly blinding year, in which millions followed Harry's every move.

The following morning, still on a high from the night before and getting back to his hotel at 4 a.m. after the exclusive after-party, he tweeted: 'Last night was the best thing I have ever done.'

The Chairman-CEO of Columbia Records, Rob Stringer, said the 90-minute set was 'almost like the biggest showcase you've ever been to' and the world's most influential music magazine, *Billboard*, declared that the gig was 'less of a proper concert and more of a victory lap from a banner year.'

The epic performance cemented their status as the top boyband in the world.

This unprecedented level of success was something no one could have predicted two years earlier – not even their mentor Simon Cowell when he signed them to his prestigious Syco label after they came third in *The X Factor*, behind Rebecca Ferguson and Matt Cardle.

Their meteoric rise to global superstardom has made music history and they have broken hearts and records along the way, landing two No. 1 albums in the States, a feat that not even the mighty Beatles could manage back in the 1960s. They have notched up a whopping 15 million record sales and their second album '*Take Me Home*' has reached the top of the charts in a staggering thirty-five countries.

Before he entered the show, Harry, an ordinary lad with a big smile and bags of charm, was singing in a small band called White Eskimo and living in rural Cheshire. He enjoyed the simple things in life. He had fun with his friends, dated girls from school and earned £3.65 an hour at the local bakery on Saturdays.

Fast-forward to 2013 and he is now a member of one of the biggest boybands in the world.

CHAPTER ONE

'They were happy days'

Long before *The X Factor* had even hit the screens in the UK, a cheeky youngster from leafy Holmes Chapel in Cheshire was entertaining his friends at school with his singing, dancing and juggling. Super-cute with straight, chocolate-brown hair, an infectious laugh, a perfect red mouth and a dimple on his right cheek, he was a natural extrovert, popular with everyone, who loved being the centre of attention. Right from the start, Harry Styles was a born performer.

Harry was born on Tuesday, 1 February 1994 in the small market town of Evesham in Worcestershire, the second child of Anne, a glamorous 25-year-old brunette, and her husband, Des, who was ten years her senior. The couple were very much in love and already had a young daughter, Gemma, who was a toddler. They were over the moon when Harry was born, completing their little family. As a baby, he had a mop of white-blond curly hair and deep blue eyes, which would later turn to sparkly green.

Harry is an Aquarius and, like his star sign, he has an expressive personality and 'an aura of kindness' about him. He is also honest and loyal.

When their new son was a few days old, Des proudly went to register Harry's birth at Bromsgrove Registration Office, where he excitedly wrote that the full name of their new little boy would be Harry Edward Styles.

Harry was still a baby when his family moved to Holmes Chapel, a quaint village in the north-west of England, 21 miles south of Manchester. With a population of just 5000 people, it had all the amenities that a young family might need, and Des and Anne wanted somewhere for their children to grow up that was warm and welcoming, with a real sense of community. Holmes Chapel fitted the bill. At his *X Factor* audition, Harry himself admitted that the area is 'quite boring' and 'not much happens there'. But he did concede with a grin that it is 'picturesque'. The village is in a delightful setting with views over unspoilt countryside and farmland.

Harry was a quick developer and his first word was 'cat'. Anne said: 'My parents had a black cat and I remember walking through the gate one day and he pointed and said "cat". It was a very proud moment.'

When he was two, Harry attended the local Happy Days nursery, which was run by the same woman who sometimes babysat Gemma and Harry when Anne and Des went out.

'They were happy days to be fair,' Harry said in the group's official book, *Dare to Dream*. He was a good baby who enjoyed playing with his toys and painting and always had one of his gorgeous smiles for the staff. He was creative from the start and would try anything new. One unusual thing he enjoyed was drawing pictures on bread with food colouring and then toasting it. He was encouraged to embrace his expressive side and was always trying to entertain those around him.

In an interview with *Now* magazine, Anne said: 'He's certainly not shy about himself. Ever since he was young he's made people smile. I always thought he'd end up on stage.'

His first day at Hermitage Primary School was a big occasion for Anne, who couldn't believe her little boy was growing up so fast. At that time, Harry's hair had grown straight and turned light brown; he wouldn't get his trademark curls back until he was twelve. Dressing him in the uniform of grey trousers, white polo shirt and navy jumper, she walked him in to the reception class and stayed for a few hours to help him feel comfortable in his new environment. He settled in immediately and Anne left him playing happily, though he was quite bemused by some of the other children, who were crying for their mums. Wherever he was and whatever he was doing, he approached it with a laid-back attitude and enjoyed himself. Other youngsters were drawn to him and he made friends quickly and easily.

Harry said: 'I used to be friends with girls as well as boys. I wasn't one of those boys who thought girls were smelly and didn't like them; I was kind of friends with everyone.'

Harry's best friend at the time was a boy called Jonathan, who has remained a close confidant. Harry calls him regularly and sees him when he is back home in Cheshire.

Des and Anne both worked hard and Harry had a comfortable upbringing. The family enjoyed regular holidays, including a fun trip to Florida. However, behind the scenes, Anne and Des' marriage was breaking down. After long and painful talks, they decided to split up. Harry was seven and completely unaware of the problems his parents had been having.

In an interview with *The People*, Des described 'the worst day of his life' when he told Harry and his sister Gemma that he and Anne weren't going to be together any more. As they broke the news to their children, who sat in front of them in their lounge Harry, who wasn't usually one to cry, broke down in tears.

Harry also admitted in *Dare to Dream* that it was 'quite a weird time'. 'I remember crying about it when my parents told me they were splitting up, but after that I was alright,' he confessed. 'I guess I didn't really get what was going on properly, I was just sad that my parents wouldn't be together any more.'

To ease the pain of the split, Des remained at the family home for two years, sleeping in the spare room, saying it was 'the best way forward', before one day he finally left for good.

Harry was understandably upset but remarkably resilient as he moved with his mum and Gemma to a pub in Northwich, further into the Cheshire countryside, where Anne was the new landlady. Harry became the 'man of the house' and learned to do all the male jobs, such as dealing with hairy spiders and putting the bins out.

Again, he found it effortless making friends and teamed up with an older boy called Reg, who was the only other kid in the local area. They bonded over a mutual love of ice cream and would cycle 2 miles every day on their bikes to Great Budworth Ice Cream Farm, where Harry would devour his favourite honeycomb flavour by the bucketload. When he is home, he always visits the farm and even took the other 1D boys there when they stayed with him during the audition stages of *The X Factor*. Harry is a huge fan of the iced dessert and says if he were going to create a flavour, he would opt for gingerbread!

Despite the big changes in his life, Harry didn't misbehave as some children might – he only ever got into one fight at primary school. Instead he chose to diligently plough all his efforts into his schoolwork and sport, especially football. He also enjoyed badminton and once won a silver medal. He was a good all-rounder, and although not as academic as his older sister Gemma, he loved writing essays in English, even getting an A grade for his first attempt.

Harry would soon discover his biggest passion: being on stage. He loved acting and appeared in school plays, including playing the role of Buzz Lightyear in an adaption of

Chitty Chitty Bang Bang, where he hid from the Child Catcher in the toy store. He also acted the lead role in a play called *Barney* about a mouse who lives in a church, dressing up in a pair of Gemma's grey tights and a headband with ears glued on.

Harry loved the adrenaline of being on stage, hot under the glare of the lights and bowing at the end to rounds of applause from the appreciative audience. He said: 'The first time I sang properly was in a school production – the rush that I got was something that I really enjoyed and wanted to do more of.'

His father – who Harry still saw regularly at the weekends – used to sing to him when he was a baby and played him rock and pop songs by Elvis Presley, Queen and The Beatles in the car. Harry cites these artists as some of his earliest musical influences. After he had been showing off his vocals at home, his granddad, Brian – who Harry describes as 'the coolest guy ever' – bought him a karaoke machine so he could record himself. One of the first tracks he performed was Elvis Presley's 'The Girl of My Best Friend'.

As he grew up, his musical tastes developed and he is a big fan of Coldplay. He loves the album *Parachutes* so much that when he was fourteen he listened to it every night before he went to sleep for about two months. Another of his favourite tracks is John Mayer's 'Free Fallin' and, more recently, he said he loved Noel Gallagher's High Flying Birds. Although, like most of us, he does own some embarrassing songs and Whigfield's 'Saturday Night' is on his iPod!

It was during his first year at secondary school at Holmes Chapel Comprehensive on Selkirk Drive that he found another outlet for his singing. He became friendly with a boy called Will Sweeny, who said they instantly hit it off when they met.

Will told online magazine *Sugarscape* how it was clear straightaway that he and Harry were very similar, and in that first week they got along so well that they spent most of it at each other's houses.

Will – who plays the drums – had formed a band with his friend Haydn Morris, a guitarist, and another guy called Nick Clough, who plays bass guitar. They wanted to enter the school's Battle of the Bands competition. Initially Harry thought he would learn the bass and he started looking at guitars on the Internet, but because Nick could already play, the others asked Harry to try out as their singer. At first, he was really self-conscious and hated listening back to himself. He had only ever sung properly in the shower or in the car.

They were impressed by handsome Harry's rocky, raw voice, so they decided that he would be their new frontman. Will explained: 'You could tell he had a good voice. It needed work but so does everyone's, but you could tell he could sing. He progressed really, really well.'

The band started to rehearse together regularly after school and their favourite hits were 'Summer of '69' by Bryan Adams and 'Are You Gonna Be My Girl' by Jet, so they were the obvious song choices for the competition.

However, they were stuck on one thing: their name.

While they were all shouting out random thoughts, Harry came up with the idea of 'White Eskimo' and they all loved it. During practice Will taught Harry how to play the guitar and he also played the tambourine during some of their gigs. He can also play the kazoo.

White Eskimo's first public performance was at the school's much-hyped Battle of the Bands competition. It was held in the canteen, where all the pupils gathered to watch twelve bands go up against each another. After getting down to the final three, White Eskimo won and picked up their prize of £100 and four tracks recorded on CD for them to keep. The recordings weren't very good quality as they were done in the school's music rooms, but winning was the boost the boys needed to decide to take their musical future more seriously.

At his first audition, Harry told *X Factor* host Dermot O'Leary: 'We entered a Battle of the Bands competition about a year and a half ago. It showed me that's what I wanted to do. It was such a thrill being in front of that many people singing. It made me want to do it more and more. People tell me I'm a good singer. It's normally my mum. Singing is what I want to do and if people who can make that happen for me think I shouldn't be doing that, then it's a major setback in my plans.'

Harry clearly made a big impression on those who witnessed the school performance. A girl called Bethany Lysycia, who was in the audience, says she isn't surprised Harry has become a star.

'They were really good. Everyone was really impressed,

especially with Harry,' she said to the *Crewe Chronicle*. 'We all knew he could sing because we would see him singing in the corridors all the time.'

And Harry's head teacher, Denis Oliver, added: 'He's a popular lad. White Eskimo won Battle of the Bands here when he was in Year 10. He's performed in a lot of assemblies.'

The group, who recruited a new bassist called Jacob, began to practise regularly at Will's house every Wednesday after school. In June 2010 they landed their first proper gig – the wedding of a young couple called Martin and Claudia in nearby Sandbach, where Will lives. The group, who looked smart in black and grey suits and sharp white shirts, performed a short set with seven or eight covers, including Harry's favourite, 'Summer of '69'. At the end they played an original song that Harry and the boys had written, called 'Gone in a Week'.

While Harry's vocals were slightly off-key at times, his charisma, bouncing energy and infectious smile made the gig a huge success and the band were ecstatic at the end of the night when they were handed £160 in crisp bank notes. Harry couldn't believe his luck. It was a lightning-bolt moment: maybe he could continue doing something he loved and get paid at the same time!

The mission was then to try and forge a serious music career. Will's mum Yvette Fielding, who was famously a *Blue Peter* presenter back in the 1980s, helped them by offering advice and support on how they might break into the notoriously tough industry, where many artists worked for years and years, touring around the country, hoping to get spotted and signed up but never achieving any notable success.

However, like most teenagers, Harry didn't let his ambition detract from having fun and he took great delight in making his mates laugh by playing jokes and clowning around at every possible opportunity. Pranks included pole dancing in the playground and even mooning!

Will admitted to *The Sun* that he and Harry would often play up in public. Amongst other things they would go into the supermarket where Harry would pretend he had Tourette's by randomly shouting out. They were also told off by security and other customers for throwing items from the shelves over their head for the other to catch. Will said of his friend: 'He was always up for fun, wacky things, having a laugh, and he never cared what people thought.'

And Harry and his mates loved to dare one another to do crazy things at the many parties they went to at each other's houses.

Harry told *We Love Pop* magazine: 'At my friend's birthday party a few years ago I got dared to go and get in bed with his mum. She was asleep and she woke up when I got in, so I just ran down the stairs. She had a robe on, but I don't know if there was anything on underneath.'

And once he ran through a train station with just his boxers on!

After White Eskimo's success in the Battle of the Bands competition and their wedding gig, Harry was becoming something of a local celebrity in his small town and girls everywhere wanted to talk to him. But rather than causing any jealousy amongst his mates, they would instead wind him up by saying it was "Classic Styles". Will said, 'He's really easy to talk to – if you met him in the street, you wouldn't feel intimidated.'

Even though he is a ladies' man, it seems his first crush was never reciprocated. Phoebe Fox was the daughter of one of Anne's friends and 'the cutest little girl', according to Harry. He was quick to turn on the charm and tried to impress her by buying her a fluffy teddy bear, which matched one he owned. However, despite the setback, it seems he was a huge hit with the girls at school. He has been asked many times when he had his first kiss and Harry says he was eleven, but has never revealed who the lucky girl was.

Will told the *Daily Star*: 'I've known him since was four years old. I know it sounds funny, but even in primary school he had a few girls on the go. It was rather amusing. From Year 4, when he was about ten, Harry started with proper girl-friends. He just had this unbelievable way with girls all his life . . .'

Des also acknowledges that people everywhere were drawn to his son. He recalled in *The People* about a holiday to Cyprus that they had taken when Harry was eight years old, and how even then there would be groups of teenage girls waiting to say goodbye to him as they boarded the bus to the airport. When asked how he did it, Des commented, 'He's just got this fantastic personable demeanour. Clearly he's a bit special. It's not just his looks but he's very charming. It's like a gift . . .'

Harry was twelve when he started going out with Emilie, who he dated for a few months, and he says his first serious girlfriend was called Abi.

A girl named Lydia Cole, who was at Harry's school, told the *Crewe Chronicle* that he was her first proper boyfriend. She said: 'We all love him to bits. What you see on screen is what you get. That's Harry. He's always been charming and cheeky and fame hasn't changed him one bit.'

Another girl called Felicity Skinner also claimed that she dated Harry for just under a year when they were both fifteen and that he was 'very romantic' and 'shy', and now fans pretend to be her.

She explained how a friend of hers who lived near where Harry grew up had introduced them, and how although it was a long-distance relationship it was 'a lot of fun'. Felicity went on to say that it was 'puppy love' but that they were definitely each other's first loves. When asked why they had split up she responded by saying that they 'just drifted apart'.

Harry always went for girls' personalities, says Will, rather than how they looked. 'He talked about how a girl seemed like a nice person not what her body was like. It's what's inside the person that matters to Harry.'

He and Will used to go on double dates and buy their girlfriends Valentine presents together. Harry later admitted during a radio interview just how romantic he is: he said that one of his girlfriends had a park near her house with a bridge running over a stream, and he set up all these candles on the bridge. But when he called her she said it was too dark and she wasn't coming out. We bet she is kicking herself now!

Harry describes his home life as 'liberal' when it came to relationships and Des admits that they never had to have an awkward chat about sex.

He said: 'I never needed to sit him down and tell him about the birds and the bees. I tried to train him up as we went along. We had conversations and it was almost as though he'd say, "Yeah, Dad, I'm on board with that," rather than going all sicky and saying, "Oh, Dad, don't talk about things like that," as some kids do. He's not one to run three girls at once. He's a one-girl person when he's with somebody.'

It seems his first experiences with girls weren't without their mishaps. Talking about his worst kiss growing up, Harry said: 'It was like having an ice lolly. It was more like a cat drinking water from a bowl. Then somebody cut my lip once! She came in a bit too fast, hit my lip onto my tooth and it started bleeding. There was blood everywhere!'

And the first time anyone has sex is a big enough deal as it is, but Harry later admitted that when he lost his virginity, he was terrified he had got the girl in question pregnant.

'The first time I had sex I was scared I got the girl pregnant – that was despite the fact we were safe,' he told *OK!* magazine. 'Luckily we were fine. To get lazy and say you'll be fine is selfish. I'd never risk not wearing a condom – it's too much of a risk. You can never say it'll never happen to you but I bet most people it happens to say that. If you're not ready for a child, don't risk it.'

By the time he was dating girls properly, Harry, Anne and Gemma had moved back to Holmes Chapel, where Anne met Harry's now-stepdad Robin Twist. The couple were sensitive about Gemma and Harry's feelings but Harry always liked Robin, describing him as 'a really cool guy'. He was at his girlfriend Abi's house when Robin proposed on the spur of the moment one Christmas Eve, while they were watching an episode of the TV soap *Coronation Street*.

Harry was really happy for his mum and has always maintained a particularly close relationship with Anne. She calls him her 'little Mummy's boy' and maintains that he gives her great hugs because he is so caring.

Harry's home life was very relaxed and his friends came over as and when they liked. Will told *Sugarscape* how welcoming Anne had always been to him and his other friends, and how even when Harry wasn't home she would still sometimes cook his tea. He revealed that Harry's mates all got on well with Anne and they gave her the nickname Foxy Coxy – which is now her Twitter name – because as well as being 'a really nice lady' she is also very pretty.

Alongside schoolwork and his band practice, Harry was happy to earn some pocket money and for two and a half years he worked at the local bakery, W. Mandeville, every

Saturday. He was paid £3.65 an hour for sweeping the floor, entertaining the older women who worked there and charming the customers with his good looks. There was also another bonus – on his breaks he would enjoy one of the shop's special brunch pasties, containing bacon, eggs, sausage and cheese, followed by a vanilla custard slice or millionaire's shortbread.

His boss, Simon Wakefield, revealed that it was his husky voice that the women loved and that they always had a rush of female customers when Harry was working. Simon told the BBC: 'He was good to have about. There was always a good atmosphere when he was around.'

While he worked Harry used to burst into song in front of the other staff. Simon added: 'We always knew he had it in him, we got used to it. It wasn't even round the back, it was in the front.'

However, much as he enjoyed the work at the bakery and his life in Holmes Chapel, Harry was determined to hit the big time. Shows like *Pop Idol*, which Harry watched as a child, and *The X Factor*, which started in 2004, were huge, with audiences of over 10 million regularly tuning in on a Saturday night to see wannabes fight it out to land plum record deals. Harry had watched from his front room while the likes of Eoghan Quigg, JLS and Joe McElderry became stars overnight, grabbing newspaper headlines and scores of female fans.

To audition in front of the mighty Simon Cowell and the other *X Factor* judges would be a dream come true and confirm to him whether he had the talent to succeed in a notoriously difficult industry. He told his fellow White Eskimo band members that he planned to audition and they were happy for him but his nerves got the better of him. In the end, it was Anne who finally sent off the *X Factor* application form in the post – for which Harry says he will always be grateful.

After that, it was a matter of counting down the days until he went to audition for the seventh series of the hit show. Little did he know how much that fateful day in Manchester would turn his life upside down.

CHAPTER TWO

'It's one word that can change your life forever'

While picking up a £1 million record deal, including recording and promotional costs and all the trappings of fame, may be the dream of all *X Factor* entrants, it is no guarantee of success or a lifetime of stardom and luxury.

Steve Brookstein notoriously won the first series of the ITV show in 2004 but was dropped by Sony BMG just eight months later, after selling only 100,000 albums and falling out with Simon Cowell. He now sings on P&O cruises and in local Starbucks coffee houses. In 2010 he even played a Cornish pub, where tickets were sold for a measly £2.50.

But as well as the flops, there are huge hits and acts like Leona Lewis, who is hailed as one of *The X Factor*'s biggest success stories. After being crowned winner in 2006, the softly spoken star landed a No. 1 with her debut single, 'A Moment Like This', and then signed a £5 million deal in the US. She cracked the American market and topped the charts in numerous countries, racking up 20 million sales along the way.

Prior to *The X Factor* was *Popstars: The Rivals*, which created the hugely popular five-piece girlband, Girls Aloud, whose breakout star, Cheryl Cole, was said to be worth £12 million in 2012 in the *Sunday Times* Rich List. Even a relatively lesser act like Will Young, who won the inaugural series of *Pop Idol* in 2002, had a string of successful singles and albums and he has won many awards, including two prestigious BRITs.

When Harry turned up on audition day, rather than thinking about the end goal, he only had one aim in mind: getting three 'yeses' from the panel, which consisted of Simon Cowell, Louis Walsh and Nicole Scherzinger. Nicole was drafted in as a guest judge at the last minute to cover for Cheryl, who was hospitalised with malaria following a holiday in Tanzania.

Notoriously laid-back, Harry was fairly philosophical about his audition: if he made it, great; and if he didn't, he had other plans, maybe to become a physiotherapist or a lawyer. He was going to study law, sociology and business for his A-levels at college and was happy to get his head down and work hard to fulfil his goals. He felt he had nothing to lose.

He may be blasé about of lot of things, but Harry's dream

was almost in tatters before it began when he fell ill on the day before his *X Factor* audition. 'I kept being sick just before I went on *The X Factor*,' he said. 'I remember I kept throwing up and then I got really bad and I started coughing up blood.' Thankfully he was discharged from the local hospital and left without a diagnosis.

After the band formed he admitted that he got terrible stage fright and went through a period of throwing up all the time, which seems quite out of character and was always a shock to him, so perhaps his hospital dash can be put down to this. At one stage it was even rumoured that Simon Cowell roped in his close friend, hypnotist Paul McKenna, to help heal Harry's crippling case of nerves.

Like most teens he isn't a fan of early mornings but on the audition day he pulled himself out of bed at 3 a.m., while it was still pitch black outside, and his devoted mum drove him to the Trafford Centre in Manchester, where the auditions were being held. When they arrived, there was a huge queue snaking around the barriers and there were people of all ages camping out in tents. Most of them had been waiting for many hours already. The wannabes played guitars and sang chart hits to pass the time and Harry dutifully waited his turn to sign in and sing his heart out.

Audiences only see the audition in front of the judges, but the participants needed to make it through two rounds with producers before facing Simon and the other judges. Presumably Harry sailed through these on the strength of his good looks and rocky singing voice.

When Harry made his way to the first televised audition, he looked as unflappable as ever and no one would ever have guessed that he had been so unwell just a few hours earlier. Dressed in jeans, a white t-shirt, grey cardigan and scarf, he kissed Anne before walking on to the huge stage to face the 3000-strong crowd and the judging panel. He brushed his hair from his face – he had only started growing out his trademark curly hair a year before, his mum Anne revealed, saying he did it because the 'chicks dig it!'

Anne, Robin, Gemma and two friends stood backstage alongside Dermot, wearing black and white 'We Think Harry's Got The X Factor' t-shirts that they had made especially for the occasion.

Introducing himself to Simon Cowell, Harry revealed that he had always wanted to audition but had been too young. Having turned sixteen the previous February this was his first opportunity. His opening audition was 'Isn't She Lovely?' by Stevie Wonder, which he sang a cappella (without accompaniment). He was met with enthusiastic applause from the massive crowd.

Pussycat Dolls singer Nicole Scherzinger said: 'I'm really glad that we had the opportunity to hear you *a cappella* because we could really hear how great your voice is. For sixteen, you have a beautiful voice.'

However, Louis – who has managed some of the music world's most successful bands, including Westlife, Boyzone and Girls Aloud, in the past – wasn't as enthusiastic.

'I agree with Nicole. However, I think you're so young,'

he commented. 'I don't think you have enough experience or confidence yet.'

Meanwhile, Simon was adamant Louis had made the wrong call. 'Someone in the audience just said rubbish and I totally agree with them because the show is designed to find someone like you whether you're fifteen, sixteen, seventeen. It doesn't matter. I think with a bit of vocal coaching you could be very good.'

After Louis said he didn't want to put Harry through, the audience booed and then heckled loudly after being encouraged by Simon, who together with Nicole secured Harry's place in the next round and his place at Bootcamp.

The day of Bootcamp dawned at Wembley Arena in July. It was set to be as ruthless as ever. On their first morning Simon announced that by the end of the day, half of the 211 hopefuls who had made it that far would be sent home.

On arrival, the auditionees were divided into their four categories: Boys, Girls, Over 25s and Groups. None of the auditions had been aired on TV at that point, so Harry had no idea what the other singers were like and who he would be up against as he battled it out for his place in the Judges' Houses stage.

Simon told them: 'Today, you're going to be put into your categories and you're going to sing one song. There are literally no second chances today.'

Each category was given a different track to rehearse and the Boys were given Michael Jackson's 'Man in the Mirror'. By making the contestants perform the same song the judges would be able to differentiate the good singers from the great ones.

Some of the attendees who had wowed the crowds during the first phase of the show buckled under the pressure, whilst others came off stage thinking they'd nailed it when they had been out of tune. Luckily Harry put in a great performance and sailed into Day Two.

Also going through were four other singers in the Boys category: Zayn Malik, Louis Tomlinson, Niall Horan and Liam Payne.

Bradford-born Zayn was seventeen when he entered and, like Harry, he had enjoyed singing at school and had taken roles in school productions, so he decided to have a crack at auditioning for the show. He is known for his vanity, and likes to spend hours in front of the mirror, perfecting his look.

Louis, eighteen, from Doncaster, already had a head start in the world of showbiz. He had taken small TV roles, including one in a drama called *If I Had You*, and starred in the series *Waterloo Road*. He had also appeared in school productions, including playing Danny Zuko in *Grease*. And like Harry he joined a band at school (called The Rogue), entered music talent competitions and performed local gigs. He shares Harry's energy and outgoing personality and would eventually become his closest confidant in the group.

Niall, sixteen, auditioned in Dublin, having travelled from

the small town of Mullingar, where he lived. He had also participated in school productions and had entered a local Stars in Their Eyes competition, where he sang the Jason Mraz track, 'I'm Yours'. Inspired by the success of previous *X Factor* winners like Joe McElderry, who seemed to gain overnight stardom, he had decided to enter the night that the Geordie singer won the sixth series of the show. He amused the crowds on the day he auditioned, bringing along his guitar and singing Justin Bieber's 'One Time' while he waited. The girls standing next to him were so impressed that they filmed him.

Finally, Liam from Wolverhampton was seventeen and a natural performer and singer, taking to the microphone at a holiday camp at the tender age of five to sing Robbie Williams' 'Let Me Entertain You'. He did well at sport and was such a good runner that he had even represented the UK. He had made it through to the Judges' Houses stage two years previously in 2008 and went to Barbados to sing in front of Simon, who told him that he wasn't going to be put through, even though he looked like a 'perfect pop star'. Since then, he had been working hard taking vocal lessons and had sung alongside other big names, including Peter Andre. When they changed the minimum age from fourteen to sixteen, he was forced to wait another year before he auditioned again. He was determined to make it this time.

After celebrating that he had made it through, Harry went straight back to the Wembley hotel and relaxed with some of the other contestants. While many of the wannabes partied late into the night and got drunk, Harry enjoyed himself for a couple of hours before turning in for an early night.

The next morning, as the remaining singers were taken on to the stage, Simon and Louis said they would be taught how to dance to the Lady Gaga song 'Telephone' by the show's resident choreographer, Brian Friedman, who has worked with Britney Spears, Beyoncé and Mariah Carey.

Brian told them: 'I don't want you to be scared: what we are going to work on is your stage presence and choreography.'

After some practising, the boys started their routine in front of Simon and Louis and some of them – including Harry – nailed it, but the judging duo realised that they were missing one singer: Zayn.

This was the first time the viewers had met Zayn, because his TV audition was never televised, and he was struggling with the dance moves. He explained: 'I seriously don't want to do it because I hate dancing, and I've never done it before and I feel like an idiot on the stage with other people, who are clearly better than me, and I just feel like an idiot – I'm not doing it.'

Instead of telling him that if he was giving up so easily, he must leave, Simon refused to allow Zayn to make a huge mistake and told him: 'Zayn, why aren't you out there? Why aren't you out there? You can't just bottle it, you can't just hide behind here! Zayn, you are ruining this for yourself. I'm trying to help you here. So, if you can't do it now, you're never going to be able to do it, right? Come on, let's go and do it!'

Rather than being cruel and making him perform the routine on his own, he put Zayn together with Harry, who was an accomplished dancer and looked the part in a purple hoodie and high-tops, and a few of the other boys, who muddled through together.

By that point Harry was becoming more optimistic about his chances and told the cameras: 'As you go through Bootcamp, you kind of realise how big the prize is, so being here for the last few days has made me realise how much I wanna stay – I really don't want to go home now.'

On the following day, the glamorous Nicole Scherzinger joined the panel of judges once again to help cover for Cheryl, who was still recovering from malaria. Following her illness and subsequent collapse, Cheryl had a period in intensive care. This had sent the schedule into chaos. Even though it was reported Simon had moved the dates of Bootcamp back in the hope that the Girls Aloud singer would recover in time to attend the live shows, she was still seriously unwell and recuperating at home. She later admitted how serious it was – Cheryl was so poorly she had been 'hours from death'.

Nicole, who had backed Harry from the start, was particularly excited to be back to help out because she would help select who would go through to the Judges' Houses stage. With Cheryl away and the fourth judge, Dannii

Minogue, on maternity leave with her first baby, they decided not to have a live element to Bootcamp as they had done in previous years. Harry was understandably disappointed because he got a boost from the crowd when he was in Manchester, and many fans of the show were also left disappointed that they couldn't see the wannabes in action.

On Day Three, the participants were given a list of forty songs to choose from. Harry picked the Oasis hit 'Stop Crying Your Heart Out' and sang well with his normal energy.

He later told TV documentary *One Direction: A Year in the Making* that he knew he had picked a 'safe song' – one in which he wouldn't stumble over high notes and make a fool out of himself – and that he regretted it. He said: 'When I look back on it now, it's really annoying because my performance was so boring.'

Each act took to the stage, performed their track and left without any comment from the judges, not knowing if they'd done enough to get to the next stage.

On the final day, 23 July, it was decision time and Louis, Simon and Nicole gathered to discuss who would make it through. Normally six acts would be chosen but it was decided that they would pick eight acts for each category because Cheryl and Dannii had missed the first auditions and Bootcamp stages and Simon didn't want them to moan. Nicole then suggested the Over 25s became the Over 28s, so the talented singers could be more evenly spread among the categories. With Polaroid pictures in front of them of the acts that were still there, they spent hours deliberating as to who they wanted to work with. Slowly they whittled them down to the chosen few.

Thirty boys remained when they were called on stage, and you could feel the tension crackle in the air. The names were read as follows: 'John Wilding. Nicolo Festa. Paije Richardson. Aiden Grimshaw. Marlon McKenzie. Karl Brown. Matt Cardle.'

With seven acts already through, there was only one place left and Harry's heart was in his mouth; he really, really wanted this opportunity. However, it wasn't to be: the final name was Tom Richards.

It was a huge shock for Harry, who was left absolutely shattered, wiping his tears with his beanie hat, saying: 'I'm really gutted.' The prospect of going home to Cheshire and back to school when he had got so far wasn't one that Harry relished.

Liam, who had been a favourite up until that point, also cried, sobbing to Dermot: 'I just don't want to go home, I just don't want to go.'

It looked as if Harry's dream was over. He was thinking about calling his mum to let her know before packing up his stuff and leaving when suddenly, in a shock twist at the eleventh hour, he was called back by a member of staff, along with Zayn, Niall, Louis and Liam, and four girls who had also failed to make it through: Esther

Campbell, Rebecca Creighton, Sophia Wardman and Geneva Lane.

Producers told them they would be needed for more interviews and for Harry it still didn't click what might happen when he saw himself standing alongside four other good-looking young boys in the wings. He didn't dare imagine that he might be offered a second chance as he nervously shuffled on stage with the others, looking shell-shocked.

Nicole told them: 'Hello. Thank you so much for coming back. I know, judging by some of your faces, that this is really hard. We have thought long and hard about it and thought about each of you as individuals and felt you are too talented to let go of. We think it would be a great idea to have two separate groups.'

Simon told them it was a 'lifeline'. 'You have to work, ten, twelve, fourteen hours every single day and take this opportunity,' he said. 'You have a real shot here, guys.'

Harry couldn't believe his ears and fell to his knees with glee, while an excitable Niall jumped on his back in delight. He later summed up his joy with the words: '[It went from] being the worst feeling in my life to the best.'

In an interview with *Rolling Stone*, Simon admitted that even though their separate auditions were good, as the competition progressed they didn't make such an impact. But when they were sent home, he had a gut feeling it was the wrong decision and there might be another way forwards for them. So they summoned them back and put them together as a group.

The boys flew backstage to meet the other successful acts and Harry gave Aiden Grimshaw a huge hug – the pair had become good friends over the days they had been in Wembley. Harry had decided immediately that he would join the group – it was a no-brainer for him and a chance to make it to the live shows – but Liam took a bit longer making his decision because he had worked hard to build his profile as a solo artist. However, the following morning he told the other boys that he was on board. The line-up was complete.

In the band's official book, *Dare to Dream*, Harry described the event as a 'blur' and said: 'I'd spoken to Louis, Zayn and Niall at Bootcamp and remember thinking, "This is going to be a lot of fun."' Harry had apparently first met Louis in the bathroom when he was washing his hands. He looked up into the mirror and spotted Louis behind him, grinning and waving. Harry smiled back and the boys hit it off. Harry later joked that it was 'love at first sight'.

The first time the group got together properly, the only thing they could think of was what they would wear. Liam said: 'The first time we all stood together and talked about what we were gonna do, we stood in a circle and we were, like, "Let's dress like Niall," because we liked his shoes. That was the first conversation we had. That was the only worry we had.'

Harry added: 'And then we just thought: how are we gonna meet up, 'cos Niall lives in Ireland. And then we were getting each other's numbers and then we were talking about meeting up.'

Shortly afterwards the judges found out who would be mentoring each category. Simon – who favoured the Girls and then the Boys – wasn't happy at all when he was told that he had got the Groups, while Dannii had landed the Boys, Cheryl the Girls and Louis the Over 28s. When Simon was told over the phone by a producer which group he would be getting, he replied with his trademark sarcasm: 'Thank you for repaying all my hard work this year.' On finding out Cheryl and Dannii's groups, he said: 'I can't believe it – they don't turn up to the auditions. Two words: stitch up!' If only Simon had known then what he knows now: that 1D would turn into global superstars and make him a fortune.

Meanwhile, the boys were delighted that they had Simon as their mentor. Speaking in the band's first book, *Forever Young*, Harry said: 'We all went mad, and the next moment we were laughing our heads off when he said, "You had that dreaded thought it could have been Louis, right?" We would have been happy with any of the four judges but I think secretly everyone wants Simon to be their mentor.'

Even though the boys found out in July that they had made it through, they had a long time to wait until the programme was shown on TV in the autumn, and they were told to keep it a secret. Harry was forced to delete his Facebook account because his friends might have realised and written their congratulations on his wall. His mum had previously said he was a big fan of the social networking site and, like many boys his age, would be on it chatting to friends every night until 'God knows when'.

Harry, Zayn, Liam, Niall and Louis knew they had to work hard to gel as a group. After going back to their respective homes for a few days, they decided to go and stay at Harry's family's house, where there is a bungalow at the bottom of the garden. It was just one large room but had space enough for a few blow-up beds and their stuff and was the perfect place for them to get to know each other better. They had a lot to achieve in a short space of time, so Anne and Robin left them to their own devices.

They kicked a football around the garden, swam in the outdoor pool, and sat around and sang pop hits while Niall accompanied them on the guitar – they admit that much of the singing at this time was in unison. They all put money into a kitty for food and when they were peckish, they got Louis, the oldest member of the group, to drive them to KFC for chicken and chips. They later acknowledged how important this time was for them to relax, and just sing whatever they wanted without any other influences. Zayn was the last to arrive and it took him a while to settle but once he had loosened up, he slotted in perfectly.

As well as getting to know each other, the boys needed to tackle one important task: to decide on a name for the band. They knew that a memorable name would give them a much-needed head start with the voting public when the live shows started. Harry, who clearly has a knack for thinking up new monikers, suggested One Direction, saying they all wanted to go the same way – to the top! The rest of the boys loved it; their bandname was decided.

As the week went past, the bungalow started to resemble a student flat and Anne later joked on Radio 1 that she still wanted to know who broke the leg of a chair while they were there. 'It got all rock and roll,' she laughed. 'They would sit around the fire pit in the chairs, just chilling. Generally getting to know each other and getting on with some work really . . . and breaking chairs. Boys will be boys.'

It was to be the start of a brilliant relationship with each other. The lads got on famously. Harry felt most at ease with Louis immediately, describing him as 'very similar'. The two have become extremely close.

Louis himself later said: 'It could have gone so wrong. There could have been just one person in the group who didn't gel or wanted to do things differently. Luckily there isn't.'

Harry felt so at ease with his new pals that he stripped off naked for 'banter'. This was the first time he took his clothes off but it would be one of many – all the *X Factor* finalists would be in for a treat over the weeks! He also always sleeps naked, saying that 'it's liberating'.

He told *The Sun*: 'I have great memories . . . especially of all the times I went naked. Stripping off is very liberating. I feel so free . . . no one seemed to mind. My confidence came out in my nakedness.'

Louis told *Celebs on Sunday* magazine: 'Harry likes to pull his trousers down. You do, Harry, you're always getting your bum out. I've been asleep before and Harry has hit me round the head with his penis. It actually wrapped around my whole face. Who wouldn't be envious of that?'

Liam later divulged that Louis soon established himself as the elected leader of the group. As the eldest and most out-going and chatty, he took calls from the show's producers to discuss details of what would be in store for them over the coming months. The rest of the boys soon found their place in the 1D family: Liam as Daddy Direction because he is the sensible one; Niall the cute one; Zayn the most vain and mysterious; and last but by no means least, Harry, the flirty and charming one.

The boys boarded a plane to Simon's villa in Marbella on the Costa Del Sol, where they would get to know one other even better over the course of a week's stay. The girl con-testants had gone to Sandbanks, Poole, where will.i.am was on hand to help Cheryl pick her finalists. Sharon Osbourne assisted Louis in picking the Over 28 singers in Limerick, Ireland, while Natalie Imbruglia travelled to Melbourne with Dannii Minogue to select the best of the Boys.

It seems the boys had got lucky again; they were blown away by Simon's stunning mansion, which boasted twenty bedrooms, three huge swimming pools, a luxury cinema and a state-of-the-art gym. It was costing the music boss a reported £15,000 a week to rent. Harry had been used to living in a lovely home but this was impressive even by his standards.

There were reports that some of the hopefuls not only woke Simon up when they arrived but that they caused thousands of pounds worth of damage, drinking his vintage champagne and the Sapporo beer that he had flown in from Japan, as well as covering some of the expensive antique and designer furniture, including a £5000 Persian rug, in sand and rainwater.

Simon told reporters: 'Yes, they did wake me up. To teach them a lesson, any damage to the villa will have to be paid out of their first royalty cheque – if they make it.'

Whether or not the boys had a part to play in the antics they also worked hard, practising their songs endlessly for what they knew would be one of the most important auditions of their lives. In their free time they ate pizza, went swimming in the sea, took dips in the villa's pools and messed about in the glorious sunshine.

However, plans didn't run smoothly after Louis was stung by a sea urchin while he was swimming on audition day. He was rushed to the local hospital, leaving his bandmates anxiously wondering if they should perform as a four-piece.

Liam explained to the cameras: 'For us that's really bad as we haven't had much time to practise as we've only just got together as a group. I hope he's back as we really do need him.'

Harry added: 'The clock is ticking and it's getting closer and closer to our performance so we're just waiting around and hoping he turns up.'

Thankfully Louis arrived back in time for the group's performance – a cover of Natalie Imbruglia's hit, 'Torn'. The boys were nervous as they knew they could so easily be dropped at this stage, but they were determined to give it their best shot. Liam sang the verse and Harry belted out the chorus, while Louis and Niall harmonised and Zayn finished the song.

After the boys had walked away, not knowing how they had done, Simon commented: 'They're cool, they're relevant,' to his good friend and ex, Sinitta, who was helping him decide who to put through. He acknowledged that they looked nervous but he and Sinitta both agreed Simon's decision would be a hard one. Later the music boss admitted that he knew the band was 'something special' and they blew him away.

When he was asked by *Rolling Stone* at what point he first realised the band could be massive, he confessed it was during this audition and that he immediately knew he wanted to put them through. As well as getting along brilliantly, he loved the fact they worked out the arrangements themselves and were full of fun. He said: 'The second they left we jumped out of our seats and said, "These guys are incredible!" They just had it.'

Typical Simon! But the boys certainly fell for his poker face and were desperate to know their fate.

Harry told the cameras: 'Your hunger for it grows and grows as you get through each stage of the competition. It's just the biggest stage to be told "yes" or "no" ... it's one word that can change your life forever because it won't be the same if you get a "yes" and if you get a "no", then it's straight back to doing stuff that kind of drives you to come here in the first place."

Simon went away to deliberate which of the eight acts to put through and admitted that he only made up his mind in the 'final minute' before the cameras started rolling, although it is crystal clear now that the boys' position in the live shows had always been safe and his indecision must have been about his other acts.

The following morning all the boys were up early, eager to hear what Simon's final judgement would be, but it wasn't until the afternoon that the music boss called each act in one by one to deliver his verdict, so they spent a nervous few hours trying to pass the time in the sun.

When the life-changing moment by the poolside finally came, Simon told them: 'My head is saying it's a risk and my heart is saying you deserve a shot. And that's why it's been difficult so I've made a decision. Guys, I've gone with my heart, you're through.'

Harry – who had tears in his eyes – immediately ran over to Simon, hugging him tightly, followed by Niall and Zayn who came in for a giant group cuddle. Harry was ecstatic: they had done it!

From the beginning, Simon thought Harry had something special and different about him, telling ITV2's *Xtra Factor* host, Konnie Huq: 'I would say you're drawn to Harry's personality. He's very charming and seems to be the one person who would be the easiest to talk to.'

During the flight home the boys struggled to keep their delight in check, as they were travelling with the acts that had been told they hadn't made it and were trying to be sensitive to their feelings. They knew that it could so easily have been them who were sent packing.

There would be another big test too – Harry could tell his family but no one else. It would be months before it became public knowledge and Harry had to sign a confidentiality agreement, along with the other boys and anyone who worked on the series, forbidding them to talk about who had made it through to the live shows.

Harry headed back to Holmes Chapel briefly and the other lads went their separate ways. He caught up with his family and tried to behave as normally as possible around the village, so no one suspected anything. After borrowing some money from Anne, he went to buy himself a whole new wardrobe of clothes for the live shows, including items from his favourite labels, Jack Wills, Hollister and Topman. He wanted to look his best when he headed down to London.

The day before he moved in to the *X Factor* house his first audition was shown on TV. All his friends congratulated him and he had to try not to give anything away – presumably telling them to watch the show to see if he got through to the next stages. Even at this point girls were starting to show an interest in him and he later admitted that when he went to a local pub with a friend, he was shocked when a girl gave him her number on the way out.

The news that he would become a TV star was eventually leaked to the press and even though people asked him, Harry had to remain quiet, but he was bursting to tell everyone and anyone: he was going to the live finals!

CHAPTER THREE

'I really wanted to win. I thought that we needed to win'

By 2010, *The X Factor* was in its seventh year. Simon Cowell, the impresario behind it, was keen to keep its immense popularity going, so he was hoping that small changes would keep it fresh. First he hired glam stylist Grace Woodward to help revamp the look of the finalists with more 'high fashion' and designer labels on show. He also sacked vocal coach Yvie Burnett, who had been working on the series for five years. She was gutted but her replacement didn't last long. Simon apologised and she was asked back.

She loved 1D and told the *Daily Record*: 'They look like stars and act like stars – they have got absolutely everything.'

Later in the show she pulled a prank on Harry and the

boys during rehearsals and claimed that the show was a fix and they would be leaving that night. Radio 1 DJ Chris Moyles, who was also there, played along with it and a confused Harry asked: 'Are we leaving the competition tonight?' However, they soon let him in on the joke.

Simon, who was making plans to launch the show in the US, also revealed he was fed up with listening to acts' sob stories and then seeing them being voted in on the strength of their personal story, rather than their talent.

He said: 'I banned the word journey because that was a key part of it all. We got too much of this "I'm doing it for my mum who broke her ankle" nonsense. I never bought a David Bowie album when I was seventeen because Bowie was talking on *Top of the Pops* about going on a journey. I don't want this to be a popularity competition. I think it is important that it remains a talent competition.'

He was also furious and threatened legal action when the final twelve acts were leaked online – firstly on *Digital Spy* and then on the *Radio Times* website, who were quickly forced to take it down. They were: 1D, FYD and Belle Amie for the Groups; Rebecca Ferguson, Cher Lloyd and Katie Waissel for the Girls; Aiden Grimshaw, Matt Cardle and Nicolo Festa for the Boys; and John Adeleye, Storm Lee and Mary Byrne for the Over 28s. To liven up proceedings, Simon also allowed the judges to pick some wildcard acts and the lucky chosen few were Diva Fever for the Groups, Treyc Cohen for the Girls, Paije Richardson for the Boys, and Wagner Carrilho for the Over 28s.

The new *X Factor* house was a Spanish-style £3.5 million mansion on an exclusive private road in Hyver Hill, Borehamwood, Hertfordshire. It was rented out to the show for £50,000 per week – a sum hugely inflated from the £25,000 asking price. The 2009 house in Hampstead had been mobbed throughout the series by local schoolchildren who disrupted the neighbours, including the Chinese ambassador, with noise, and lewd graffiti on the perimeter wall, so in 2010 insiders were sworn to secrecy about the location. As always, the news found its way into the public domain. However, it wasn't easy for followers to access the house because it was on a secluded road, among thick woodland. Producers hired two guards to watch the seven-bedroom property around the clock.

The boys were to live together in one room, which Harry joked was 'the worst room in the house'. It was tiny, with two sets of bunk beds, a single bed and a number of wardrobes for all their clothes. After they unpacked their numerous suitcases, the room stayed a tip throughout the entire show – and Louis was branded the messiest. Niall even admitted he cleaned up after him a few times. The girls from Belle Amie were so disgusted that they tried to tidy the room once and Konnie Huq described it as a 'pigsty'!

The boys had their own bathroom, so they didn't share with the girls, but that was also extremely messy, with boxer shorts all over the floor and open cartons of orange juice sitting on the side of the bath. There were some bizarre reports that Simon supplied them with bathroom luxuries and Harry would be spending a penny in style, after The Designer Toilet Roll Company, who supply Simon with his £10-per-roll black toilet paper at home, were asked to deliver their best tissue prints to the house!

Even though the house had been trashed during the previous year, Simon Cowell gave the finalists his blessing to 'be their age and do what they like'.

He said: 'You have got to have some sort of control in there, but at the end of the day you want to have the personalities through so it's fun. They are entering the music business for all the right reasons, and that is not to sit in the library 'till three in the morning.

The first night they moved in, the contestants all sat together in the beanbag room, which contained a huge TV, jukebox and a big piano. Matt strummed on his guitar and everyone sang along. During their downtime over the weeks the boys spent quite a lot of time in there playing on the Nintendo Wii or having a round of table tennis.

Regardless of space within the huge house, at night the boys were still living in cramped quarters and were going to have to get used to each other's less than desirable habits, including Louis' extreme messiness and Harry's snoring and talking in his sleep – they even had to tell him off a few times! They would also have 'bonding' incidents.

In the early days in the house poor Harry got food poisoning. Niall told *X Magazine*: 'The other night we'd got some food in but Harry felt a bit sick. He ran into the toilet but I was doing a poo at the time. He's shouting at me, "Get out the way, get out the way", but I can't move because I'm on the loo. He ends up being sick into the bath. It turned out he burst blood vessels in his neck and he had to go to the doctor. He'd got food poisoning.'

Liam admitted he found it hard sharing with the lads as they were so noisy and tensions started to emerge but laid-back Harry always just rolled with it – and unlike a group of girls, the boys forgot their squabbles and got on with the monumental task in hand: preparing for the live shows.

The first week's theme was Number Ones and together with Simon the boys decided on the Coldplay hit 'Viva la Vida'. As they prepared backstage for their first live performance, all the boys were extremely nervous about how it would play out. However, as soon as they stepped from behind the famous doors in the studio and started singing in front of millions of viewers at home, they were on cloud nine. Life would never be the same again. Harry later said this initial performance was one of his *X Factor* highlights.

'When we walked in and saw the studio for the first time, then when the five of us stood behind the doors for the first time on the live show, for that first song – for me that was the best moment,' he explained. 'That was where we were actually doing it, the real thing, for the first time. That was a big moment.'

Zayn had problems with coming in on time during rehearsals and he was terrified that he would ruin it for the others, but on the night he was fine and they gave a convincing performance.

Louis told them they were 'gelling' – arguing that it was his idea to put them together. He said: 'Boys, I think you could potentially be the next big boyband but you have a lot of work to do.'

Dannii called them 'the perfect band', Cheryl also felt they had the ingredients of a great group, although she thought they needed more time, while Simon told Louis they'd rewind the tapes to see whose idea it was for the boys to be put together, as it was definitely his – and said that the performance was 'brilliant'.

He said: 'We took a risk, and I've got to tell you, what is impressive about that was when you started to screw up: one of you in the end, Liam stepped in, you brought it back together. That's what boys do.'

The boys' relationship with Simon was growing and they had already started to see him as something of a surrogate-uncle figure. They teased him mercilessly. It had been his fifty-first birthday that week and they gave him a birthday card with £2.50 in it – 50 pence from each of them. 'He can buy whatever he wants with it,' Harry quipped.

Fun aside, it was a faultless start – Nicolo Festa received the lowest number of public votes so left automatically and then FYD departed after the sing-off. 1D really started to feel that it was a possibility that they could be in the competition for the long haul.

However, the nerves really hit Harry in Week Two. It was Heroes week and they had planned to sing Kelly Clarkson's 'My Life Would Suck Without You'. During the soundcheck, Harry felt so sick that he thought he might throw up and he was forced to miss the whole rehearsal. Vocal coach Savan Kotecha and choreographer Brian Friedman agreed Harry should sit it out. He was sent to the doctors but the bosses felt that it was probably just a bad case of nerves.

Harry said: 'I've never had stage fright before that has prevented me performing, which is why it has been strange for me because it has never happened to me like that before.' Luckily he managed to conquer his fears when the cameras started rolling and put in a brilliant performance.

Dannii told them: 'I have to say, you are five heartthrobs. You look great together and Harry, whatever nerves you have, I'm sure that your friends and you will stick together.'

Cheryl added: 'I can't even cope with how cute you are – seriously I can't. I just want to go over and hug them, in a nice way. You're so sweet, I'm watching the whole time thinking, "This is adorable."'

Simon declared that they were 'the most exciting pop band in the country today', while the girls went crazy, especially for Harry, who played down his previous stage fright and lapped up the attention, bursting with adrenaline.

Again, two acts were eliminated: Storm Lee immediately on the public vote and Diva Fever after the sing-off.

The following week the group got a taste of how their lives might be in the future, when they were mobbed by overzealous, screaming fans as they arrived for rehearsals at the Fountain Studios in Wembley. Harry, in particular, was besieged by girls who grabbed his checked shirt, demanded his picture and asked for his autograph. As the series progressed the fans would fearlessly hang off the security fences surrounding the studio and lie on the pavement in an attempt to get a glimpse of their new idols. Everywhere Harry went there were cameras flashing and girls asking for pictures – one fan even wanted him to sign her big toe!

Typically, Harry's mum Anne said he was 'taking it in his stride'. Talking to *Star* magazine, she explained: 'It's been a big confidence boost for him. I can't imagine what it must be like for him being just sixteen and having girls screaming at him. I think it must be rather scary.' She also said that she didn't think it would change him and that his family would bring him firmly back down to earth if he did let his new-found fame go to his head – a tactic the boys said they would use with one another if any of them were showing diva tendencies.

1D were also met by hordes of girls when they made a visit to Topman on Oxford Street, where they got to choose a free outfit, which they loved. Brands are always desperate for celebs to wear and endorse their products and this would be the first of many free things they would be given.

While they were at the famous shopping mecca, journalists flocked around to fire questions at them and Niall revealed that although they had the X factor on stage, Harry certainly didn't have it in the kitchen. He said: 'Harry almost burned the house down the other day. He was cooking pizzas and burnt them to a crisp. But we ate them anyway because we hate wasting food.'

And Matt Cardle added that Harry shocked the other members of the house after coming downstairs wearing 'nothing but a golden thong'. The ex-painter and decorator said: 'It was proper minging.' Harry later revealed that this was his 'party trick' and he liked to wear the item after he was given it by one of his friends. His love of stripping off wouldn't just be in the confines of the *X Factor* house: even Cheryl later confessed that she had seen Harry in his boxer shorts!

As the boys' popularity was becoming increasingly clear, there were rumours that 1D were Simon's favourites because he had spotted their huge potential. Craig Saggers, a member of Diva Fever, who had been voted off, told *Now* magazine: 'He only cares about One Direction. He sees pound signs when he looks at them.'

And Belle Amie's Sophie Wardman moaned to Viking FM that it was always much harder for the girl groups than boybands. She said: 'You could put the boys out there in bin bags and sing "Baa Baa Black Sheep" and they'd go through with flying colours. I think it's just a lot easier for them.'

Interestingly though, whilst the other mentors freely

handed their acts their phone numbers for them to call if they needed help or advice, Simon refused to give his to the boys. After they gave out Matt's digits to 7000 fans via a Twitcam as a joke, he was nervous about what they might do with his number. He did eventually pass it over after he signed them, and they rang him up putting on Brummie accents and telling him his trousers were too high.

Every week followed the same pattern: on the Sunday night preparations were already being made for the following week. Simon and the other judges were given a list of possible songs to choose from, then once a rough decision was made he would brief Brian Friedman on his 'vision' for the chosen song – whether he wanted a big dance number with lots of backing singers or a more pared-down production.

On the Monday the boys would run through some different song choices with Savan, who said it was all about 'experimenting' with various tracks, and everyone on the team would give their opinion until a firm choice was made.

Tuesday would see 1D spending only around half an hour with Brian, working out their moves for the night, and Grace would brief her team of five stylists on what looks they needed to find for the show, although the boys' fashion choices were always fairly straightforward in comparison to the girls, who often wore expensive designer dresses.

The next big day in the schedule would be Thursday, when Simon got together with the boys at the studio in

Wembley for rehearsals and soundchecks. This would be the first time the mentors would see their various acts perform the chosen music alongside the production that Brian had created.

There would be another early start on Friday when 1D would run through their song again on the stage, this time with backing dancers and any special effects, and the cameras would be choreographed to follow them so they could 'look down the camera'.

Saturday, of course, was show day and they would see the make-up team and stylist and get 10-minute facial massages before they had their looks sorted out. 'One Direction are usually the first bums on seats,' said make-up artist Liz Martins.

Adam Reed was the show's hairdresser and Gemma, who used to cut Harry's hair for him at home, was banned from doing it as soon as the live shows started. Initially he left it to grow until cutting it before Week Eight. Adam said Harry had the 'best hair' – and that unsurprisingly loads of people had started coming into his salon asking for Harry's curls.

At 5.30 p.m. on Saturday, Simon made any last-minute changes in a meeting with the whole team in his luxurious dressing room, and then it was show time.

The boys sailed through Week Three's Guilty Pleasures theme with Pink's 'Nobody Knows' after a midweek song change by Simon, who felt the original choice wasn't working for them. They only had one full day to rehearse but pulled a great performance out of the bag.

Louis said: 'You just have to walk out on stage: everybody's screaming, it's like five Justin Biebers! This band, you're really getting your act together. I think you are the next big pop band.'

Dannii said they were 'living the dream and loving the dream and you're letting everyone in on that with you,' and Cheryl told them: 'You are my guilty pleasure.' Along with the rest of the country, she was starting to fall in love with Harry Styles.

Walking off stage, Harry smiled: 'The comments were absolutely brilliant. For us to keep proceeding in the competition, we have to get better every week.' He was determined, along with the other 1D boys, to practise until they were note perfect and it paid off. John Adeleye was voted out after a sing-off against Treyc Cohen.

The following week they were lucky enough to have a trip to the ghoulish London Dungeon as it was the week of Hallowe'en. They also attended a Tinie Tempah gig at Camden's KOKO club and partied in a VIP booth with Kimberley Walsh, Nicola Roberts and Chipmunk. Tinie was so happy to see them that he called them up on to the stage but as they made their way up, Liam managed to accidentally trip over and twist his ankle.

That week Harry was knocked down by a bunch of fans as he got out of the car on his way into the studio and had to be helped up by the other boys. Everyone continued to be surprised about the immense interest in the group. They were starting to realise that popping out like they had before the show would be almost impossible.

On the night, the boys pulled together for their performance of 'Total Eclipse of the Heart' for Week Four's
Hallowe'en theme, complete with vampire-like make-up
with red eyes, whited-out skin and fake blood. They didn't
put a foot wrong and came away with a clean sweep of good
comments from the panel. Louis said he loved them, Dannii
added that they were 'doing exactly what a boyband should
do' and Cheryl revealed that everyone was asking her about
them.

The following day, a tired Harry told the crew: 'Last night
felt brilliant. We got a real chance to show off our vocals and
hopefully fans at home will vote and keep us in because we
really don't want to go home now.'

Belle Amie were up against Katie Waissel in the sing-off
and when the vote went to deadlock, the girl band were
sent home, leaving One Direction as Simon's only remaining act. The competition between the judges is definitely
real rather than just for the cameras and Simon was desperate for the boys to do well. He felt that they could win
the show for him.

Harry's family were also right behind them, coming every
week to cheer him and 1D on. Gemma even tried to keep all
the wristbands she was given when she entered the studio
on her arm as a sign of support. In the end, she was running
out of space, so just kept the one from the first week.

Anne told the *Crewe Chronicle*: 'I fill up with pride every
time he's on TV. I feel incredibly proud and it's all so surreal
to see my boy on the stage. At the end of the day, he's my

little baby and there he is on stage in front of millions of people.'

American Anthems was the theme for Week Five and Harry and the boys spoke to Simon a lot about their dreams of winning and breaking America, so they settled on Kim Wilde's 'Kids in America'. The production was huge, with thirty-five colourful cheerleading dancers bounding around on stage with them.

Brian Friedman spoke about how he struggled to keep them focused in rehearsals. Talking to *The Sun*, he said: 'I always used to have to say to the boys: "One Direction? It's every direction except where I need you to be!"

'But being in a room with them and trying to maintain some level of cooperation kept me young. We'd rehearse in a gym, but when I needed them to pay attention they'd throw big yoga balls at each other's heads. That was their favourite pastime in rehearsals.'

It proved to be their strongest performance to date – Simon even gave them a standing ovation. Louis noted the hysteria surrounding them, Cheryl said how lovely they were backstage to everyone they worked with – throughout the show the boys were praised for their down-to-earth attitudes – and Dannii praised their vocals. It led to another vote of confidence by the public and Treyc became the next act to leave.

The boys were on the home straight to the final. They were constantly tired but thrilled from the excitement of their new lives.

By that point, Harry and the lads had really settled into the house, although some of the other acts were filling headlines with their behaviour. Eccentric Wagner, who kept the judges divided each week after his performances, apparently moved out of the house into a local hotel because he couldn't stand being with the others. He was reportedly difficult to live with and had been getting up at 5 a.m. to practise his martial arts.

Matt was furious with fellow contestant Katie after claims they were sleeping together appeared in the newspapers. He accused her of leaking stories to the press to try and get herself more publicity and called her 'a fame-hungry tw*t'.

Cheryl's girls – Cher, Rebecca and Katie – were also apparently at loggerheads with one another and not speaking, with rumours they were jealous about which of them was getting Cheryl's attention.

Harry never got involved in rows in house, preferring to mess around with his bandmates instead. One day he and Louis dressed up in their favourite onesies for a trip to the shops, sparking a huge fashion trend. Harry wore a bright white one and they would zip their hoods up and make a dash for it, so no one would recognise them.

The group went on a few more exciting trips outside of rehearsals that week, attending the star-studded Pride of Britain Awards, where they were humbled by stories of heroic members of the public. They also went to the premiere of *Harry Potter and the Deathly Hallows: Part 1* where they walked up the red carpet for the first time as journalists screamed their names and paparazzi cameras snapped away. Once inside, they rubbed shoulders with the likes of Daniel Radcliffe and Emma Watson, and Daniel even said he was excited to meet them.

During the week Harry continued to appreciate that while there were downsides of fame, such as the constant attention, there were also perks: with notoriety came a whole new outlook and wardrobe.

Covent Garden's Jack Wills store tweeted him saying: 'What are the rules on what you wear on the shows? If we gave you a free jw t-shirt?' Harry eagerly got back, saying: 'I can wear it J. I'll be coming in tomorrow. See you soon xxxx'

He picked up a white t-shirt with a red logo but in the end he decided not to wear it. However, he mentioned it in a fashion-themed video for the *X Factor* website, so the store got a namecheck.

The next live show, in Week Six, was Elton John-themed and the group performed their first proper ballad, 'Something About The Way You Look Tonight', a real test for any group. Harry took centre stage for the first time, singing a solo section as they stood high on the stage on clear platforms, while a montage of their faces played in the background. His voice shone through and he and Liam shook hands at the end, while Simon also got to his feet.

Louis told them they were only going 'in one direction, and that is the final'. Simon also praised the fact that they were kind to everyone who they worked with and said that he genuinely thought they were going to win.

In the results show the following night, three generations of boybands were asked to appear: JLS kicked off proceedings with 'Love You More'; Westlife then performed one of their famous power ballads, 'Safe', and Take That completed the starry line-up with a rendition of their latest hit, 'The Flood'. Harry said Take That was his favourite, calling them 'legends'.

The bands had nothing but praise for the boys. Westlife's Shane Filan told *X Magazine*: 'They're the whole package: they're good singers, they're good-looking lads and they're quite cool. They're like a band of Justin Biebers and they've got everything the girls will love.'

In a shock exit, the boys' good friend Aiden was voted off after going against Katie in the sing-off and the boys were kept on their toes – they knew the fans needed to keep voting for them and that they had to keep working at it. Zayn said: 'The competition is really really heating up.' They were gutted to see Aiden go and later campaigned successfully for him to join them on the *X Factor* tour, asking their fans to sign a petition.

In Week Seven they sang 'All You Need Is Love' by The Beatles – a band that they were increasingly getting compared to as the weeks ticked by. The song was full of complicated harmonies, so they were under a lot of pressure, but again, they delivered a really great performance. Louis said it was 'good to see the Fab Five singing the Fab Four'.

Harry particularly loved this week as lots of his friends and family came to support him, and he was able to relax and have a drink with them after the show.

The much-hyped Cher narrowly escaped eviction after performing in the sing-off against Paije, who eventually left. After the show Harry was seen cuddling Cher backstage and when a picture was posted on Twitter of them looking close, they were linked as a couple. Harry was quick to deny the rumours, saying: 'Cher's not really my type. She's a great girl. We've become good friends but that's it.'

It was not the first time there had been rumours of Cher getting together with one of the boys – earlier in the process she was said to have hooked up with Liam and there were also reports that she had been seen kissing Zayn. Niall was rumoured to be dating Sophia from Belle Amie but they too denied there was any romance between them. Louis was the only member with a girlfriend at home at that time, called Hannah Walker.

It was reported that Simon was aware that Cher was feeling fragile after weeks of negative press coverage, which began after she was put through at the Judges' Houses stage even though she messed up her song. She was picked over the hugely popular Gamu Nhengu.

Simon had apparently asked his boys to keep an eye out for her, and Harry said they were all friends. He told *X Magazine*: 'Cher's the same age as us and we all get on really well. But we have a conversation with her, it gets in the paper that there's something's going on. We're all good mates.'

Speaking to the *Mirror*, he laughed: 'We're friends with all the girls in the house. I bought Cher a pork pie, but she hasn't eaten it yet – it's still in the fridge.'

He also introduced Cher to Anne after the show, who said she was lovely and that she was jealous of her hair.

Although he was keen to deny any romance with Cher, Harry was quick to say he fancied Frankie Sandford from girlband The Saturdays. After meeting her at one of the shows, he managed to contain his awe and turn on his cheeky charm. 'I spoke to her on the way out,' he said. 'I really like girls with short hair.' Sadly for Harry, the pretty star was dating Dougie Poynter from McFly.

Girls everywhere were going crazy for Harry and, after one of the live shows, Peaches Geldof pleaded to meet the boys. It was claimed that she embraced him like a long-lost friend before begging for his telephone number, talking to him about Scientology. Harry later admitted he gave her a false set of digits.

He told the *Sunday Mirror*: 'It was weird. She seemed pretty keen on talking to me but I didn't want to give her my number. I don't need any spiritual help so I nodded along, and someone suggested I give her a fake number so I swapped around the last few digits.'

On ITV2's *Xtra Factor* Peaches told Konnie Huq: 'I spoke to my sister Tiger and she was adamant I got Harry Styles on the phone. She said, "I have to tell him I'm madly in love with him." So, Tiger, if you're watching, I'm gonna tell him. I'm gonna put in a good word for Tiger. I think One Direction is the soup of the day at my household.'

The fan base was building but there was something missing – Harry didn't have an autograph and didn't know what to write, so just wrote 'Harry' in longhand. Now, of course he has it down to a fine art!

Around this time, Harry revealed he had spoken to his parents about how his life would change now he was on the show, especially when it came to girlfriends. He was starting to feel worried about whether he would be able to trust people in the same way as before he was famous.

'I spoke to my parents about it, saying how will I know it's not about the show, and they were like, you'll know when someone genuinely likes you for who you are,' he said.

Even though Simon had said that he couldn't stop the acts getting together and he was happy for them to have some freedom, it seems show bosses had decided to take security measures to the max so finalists couldn't secretly creep into each other's rooms after dark.

FYD singer Matt Newton told *Reveal* magazine: 'You want to see the security guard that patrols the hallways. No-one is getting in and no-one is sneaking into anyone else's rooms.' His bandmate Ryan-Lee Seager added: 'When you go to the toilet at night, you get a flashlight in your face. He's at the door practically counting the minutes.'

Week Eight's rock theme saw 1D perform Harry's suggestion, one of his favourite tracks, 'Summer of '69', followed by a sensitive rendition of Joe Cocker's 'You Are So Beautiful'. The group were praised for their consistency and Harry was particularly proud when Simon revealed that Bryan Adams had been Harry's choice of song. Louis said that they had been putting in 18-hour days, rehearsing in the studios until 2 a.m., but it paid off: they were safe yet again and through to the semi-final! Katie and Wagner were going home.

They also performed the finalists' single, a cover of David Bowie's 1977 hit 'Heroes', for which they had filmed their first-ever music video. Harry got his own solo line: 'Though nothing, nothing could keep us together.'

The *Mirror* newspaper alleged that during filming, which took place in a studio in east London, Wagner tried to head-butt Harry and the pair had to be dragged apart. The spat started when Harry apparently jokingly rugby-tackled him and started a play-fight. The Brazilian didn't take too kindly to it and lunged towards him, telling him that he was an expert in martial arts. The cameras were still filming, and when Wagner was told that Harry had been doing it for the video, he was forced to apologise.

Sales for the single would go to Help for Heroes and all the finalists went to Headley Court, a rehabilitation centre for injured servicemen and women in Surrey. Harry said he felt 'really privileged' to meet some of the people who were recovering there from traumatic injuries. The contestants also did an interview with Radio 1 to promote it and when it landed the No. 1 spot, they were thrilled.

By now the tension was really kicking in, with the final five acts set to perform two more songs for Week Nine's semi-final – a club classic, followed by anything of their choice. They still felt like the show could be anyone's to win: every week the other acts, especially Matt, Rebecca and Cher, were pulling great performances out of the bag.

This was by far the hardest week in the whole of the live finals for 1D because Zayn had to rush home after his grand-dad sadly passed away. The boys rehearsed their songs without him, and also without their mentor Simon, who was ill with a bout of flu. Cheryl was drafted in to help them out, as was one of Simon's friends, Tim.

Harry was also laid low with a painful sore throat and was forced to write notes instead of speaking. Under strict instructions from Savan and Yvie, one day he arrived at rehearsals with a note hanging from his neck, which read: 'I'm on vocal rest! Can't speak. Thank you.' On the Friday he left early to see the doctor and missed the final rehearsal.

Thankfully for the group, Zayn made it back from Bradford for the Saturday, proving how much he wanted to be in the final, and the boys rallied around him.

Their first track, Rihanna's 'Only Girl (In the World)', saw them bouncing around the stage with typical energy and drive.

Louis said: 'If there is any justice you will absolutely be in the final.' Dannii called the performance 'brilliant', Cheryl said she had 'thoroughly enjoyed' mentoring them in Simon's absence, while Simon declared it was 'absolutely

perfect' but urged people to pick up the phone, so they
didn't succumb to the fate of those acts who are presumed
safe, so no one votes for them.

1D's second choice, 'Chasing Cars' by Snow Patrol, was
more soulful and sensitive and was also given the thumbs up
by all the judges. Simon said: 'Guys, Tim who's been working with you all week told me that you made a decision this
morning to get in at eight in the morning so you could give
yourselves more rehearsal time and that's what it's all about.
It's not about excuses, it's about having a great work ethic,
picking yourselves up after what was a very tough week, and
I said this before – I genuinely mean this – I am proud of you
as people as much as artists.'

Their mentor later spoke about how he grew to know
and trust the lads as the weeks went past. Simon is known
for his obsessive work ethic and the extreme pressure he puts
himself under and he liked the fact the boys also worked
hard and pushed themselves. They were exactly the sort of
group he wanted to work with in the future.

On the Sunday night, after performances from Alexandra
Burke, the cast of *Glee* and The Black Eyed Peas, they were
the final act to find out they had made it through. They
whooped with delight: they were in the final! Mary became
the twelfth person to leave after performing in the sing-off
against Cher.

In the week running up to the final, the boys' schedule was
jam-packed: they put in extra rehearsals and spent a day

travelling all over the country as they headed back to each of their hometowns to drum up support and get everyone picking up their phones to vote. They didn't go back to Ireland to Niall's home in case they got stuck over there but did do a live link with *Ireland AM* from a TV studio for their Irish supporters.

Harry was over the moon to be heading back to Cheshire, their second stop after visiting Louis' old school in Doncaster. Everywhere they looked there were home-made banners, balloons and deafening screams of 'Harry Harry Harry'. The bakery where Harry used to work was showing off special One Direction loaves of bread in the window. One fan even set up a Facebook page called 'Harry Styles works in a bakery. I would check out his buns every day.' Many fans had come from as far away as Manchester and Liverpool, braving the cold for a glimpse of their new idol.

The boys had a small party with champagne and cake with Anne and Robin, who they knew quite well from their time in the bungalow before Bootcamp. Then they headed off in a blacked-out car to whizz onwards to Wolverhampton and Bradford, where they performed for thousands more fans.

Harry said: 'It's brilliant to be home because this time next week we could potentially have won the show. Every week we're all in total disbelief that we've got through and you can see it on our faces. We didn't expect to get through the Judges' Houses stage, never mind to the final. We're absolutely loving it.'

Asked if he had a message for the people of Holmes Chapel, he said: 'Everyone's been brilliant. It's a weird and wonderful feeling to have your hometown all rooting for you. I'd like to say a huge thank you to everyone but all I can ask is that people vote for us for one more week!'

The group were also forced to deny rumours that Simon had already signed them up to his record label, begging the public to support them in the quest to become the first group to win the show.

With the big prize in sight it is traditional for *X Factor* finalists to duet with a famous star, but first up for 1D was their rendition of Elton John's 'Your Song'. Liam opened, before the spotlight shone on Harry who tackled the second verse and nailed it. Again the judges had nothing but good things to say to the fivesome.

Simon said: 'I would just like to say after hearing the first two performances tonight, Matt and Rebecca, they were so good my heart was sinking. And then you came up on stage, you've got to remember you're sixteen, seventeen years old, and each of you proved that you should be there as individual singers, you gave it a thousand per cent, it's been an absolute pleasure working with you. I really hope people bother to pick up the phone, put you through tomorrow because you deserve to be there.'

For their final song they were lucky enough to be singing 'She's the One' with Robbie Williams. None of them could quite believe that they would be up on stage with such a global superstar. It really was a dream come true for all of them. Harry, who was wearing a maroon suit, said the opportunity was 'incredible' and told Dermot: 'It's such an honour to sing with Robbie.' Simon also described it as a 'magic moment'.

Backstage, the boys hit it off with Robbie, who offered them some advice from his earlier years in Take That: he was sixteen when he joined the group and was thrust into the limelight almost overnight, much like the boys had been. He said that the boys would have disagreements and arguments but they would need to stick together and get over them quickly – something the boys definitely still do. They were initially quite star-struck but quickly relaxed as they talked to the Take That superstar.

The other finalists – Matt, Rebecca and Cher – were joined by Rihanna, Christina Aguilera and will.i.am for their duets and were equally blown away to be up on stage with such incredible talent. In the end, Cher received the lowest number of votes and became the thirteenth act to leave, so the boys were through to the final three!

On the final night, they had a group performance alongside Take That, singing their hit 'Never Forget' – something Harry said they were 'chuffed to bits' about. It seemed almost inconceivable that one night they would be singing with Robbie and the next they would be joined by the other members of one of the most famous boybands on the planet.

Some of the other finalists also joined them one last time in the studio for a rendition of Lady Gaga's 'Bad Romance' and they were happy to be reunited with the likes of Aiden, who they knew would be rooting for them.

Take That also sang their latest hit at the time, 'The Flood', as part of a promotional push. It was their first single with Robbie after he had rejoined the group a few months earlier and the boys looked on in awe.

For their last-ever *X Factor* performance 1D decided to reprise their original Judges' Houses audition song, 'Torn'. It had paid off for them once before so they hoped it would have the same effect again. The judges unanimously wished them luck, saying they deserved the title because they had worked so hard.

As all three acts stood on stage next to their mentors and holding their breath, ecstasy soon turned to agony when Dermot read that it was Rebecca and Matt going to the final sing-off.

The realisation suddenly hit that they had come third, not won as they had eagerly hoped. It was heartbreaking for them all. Tears sprang into Harry's eyes and he tried to blink them away. A million thoughts shot through his head as he tried to work out what would happen next. Would he be going back to his life in Holmes Chapel?

He described the moment in the documentary, *One Direction: A Year in the Making*. 'Some people would say, you guys don't need to win but for me it was as straightforward as we *did* need to win. I really wanted to win. I thought that we needed to win.'

Simon also looked gutted – he had expected the boys to

do better. He told the audience at home that it was 'just the beginning' for the band. Judges often say this when their acts are evicted, so whether it would prove true or not, the boys would have to wait and see. They knew Simon saw potential in them, but they hadn't won.

Going off stage Harry confessed that he couldn't stop the tears from running down his face but he was forced to compose himself to listen to Matt and Rebecca perform the final two songs, the winner's tracks. Unlike previous years, they had all recorded different winning songs to suit their different vocals. 1D had also recorded a single, 'Forever Young', which they were disappointed not to be able to perform, as they had rehearsed it and even recorded it in the studio, but they duly listened to the final two acts' songs.

When Dermot announced that the winner was Matt, they were gracious and really happy for him and urged people to buy his single. Harry also cheekily whispered to Matt, who was rumoured to be dating stylist Grace Woodward, that he would be more popular than ever with the girls, saying: 'Think how much p**** you're going to get.'

Later he laughed it off, telling Alan Carr on his show *Chatty Man*: 'Right, what happened was, it was completely innocent. Basically, me and Matt had been discussing Christmas presents for our parents – it's true – and he said he wanted to get his mum as many cats as he could. Because she liked cats, so when he won, I said, "Think how many cats you can get now!"'

He also added that he was grounded for a week for his naughty comments!

It seems his sister Gemma, who was at Sheffield Uni, was more impressed. Harry said: 'I went to see my sister a few days later and a load of her uni friends were having a party. All the guys were like: "Respect!"'

Matt also joked months later: 'P*ssygate – way to take the shine off my win, Hazza! It was all I got asked about. And it's still going.'

Figures later revealed that the result had been a fair one: One Direction had come third or fourth most weeks and Matt had topped the polls every show, apart from the first one, which Mary had won. The show has seen a record 15.4 million votes cast and Simon was delighted at its success. The final of *The X Factor* was the highest-rated television show of 2010 and the series went on to win a number of prestigious awards including the Most Popular Talent Show category at the National Television Awards.

Simon could rest happy as he headed off to his luxury holiday home in Barbados for Christmas. But what of the boys? With their future hanging in the balance, they didn't know what to think.

After the show had finished, Simon invited Harry and the others to his lavish dressing room, a grey-and-black-themed suite which contained among other things Jo Malone candles, white orchids and pictures of his hero, Frank Sinatra, on the walls. Here he would deliver the news that would seal their fate. They were still bursting with excitement but crushingly disappointed at the result.

'I've made a decision,' he said. Of course in typical Simon fashion he made the boys wait with a lengthy *X Factor*-style pause before offering them a deal with his Syco label, for a reported £2 million. He believed in them and he wanted them on board.

Harry was completely overwhelmed. He said: 'I tried to stay as calm as possible, but on the inside I was terrified. As soon as Simon told us we had a record deal I started crying and I sat there thinking, Why am I crying? If this works out it's going to totally change my life.'

Simon later admitted that he knew he wanted to sign them but rather than automatically going to his own label Syco, he allowed a number of the Sony divisions to make a presentation to try and woo them. However, in the end Syco delivered the best proposition to the boys and they decided to go with them.

Again the boys were sworn to secrecy and were only allowed to tell their families – but Harry's huge grin gave him away to those who knew him best. Even though they didn't win, this was the best possible result. 1D were going to continue.

CHAPTER FOUR

'I loved the tour so much I didn't want it to stop!'

Harry knew that, with Simon and his prestigious music label behind them, anything was possible. His days of sweeping floors at the bakery and revising at school were over, for a few months at least.

Industry insiders agreed that 1D's potential was huge. Figures started being bandied around – with some saying that they could easily make as much as £1 million in a year – and many were already describing Harry as the breakout star of the group. He had been advised not to read papers or magazines but he knew he was gaining new fans by the minute.

Speaking to *Star* magazine, PR guru Mark Borkowski said: 'One Direction are going to be big, despite not winning.

They are all good-looking, have got a bit of an attitude and have a fantastic Svengali behind them in Simon Cowell. They'll definitely be millionaires by this time next year. With the right management and material, they've got everything going for them. Harry is already a cult figure. It's all there for them.'

With a sense that they were at the beginning of a whole new life, the group excitedly packed up their belongings and moved out of the *X Factor* house the morning after the final. They checked into a west London hotel for a few days, where they had a number of exciting meetings to plan their future. During this time they attended the official *X Factor* wrap party at London's Studio Valbonne, dressed in smart suits, and celebrated with all the cast and crew from the show who had become like family to them over the weeks. In a strange way, it felt like the end of an era.

Then they headed home in their separate directions, which must have felt very weird because they had been living in one another's pockets for weeks. Simon apparently gave them £8000 'pocket money' to start with and this was more money than Harry had ever dreamed of having at one time. He didn't know where to start when it came to spending it.

Most of all, though, Harry couldn't wait to get back to some kind of normality for a few days. He planned to relax and put his feet up, eat some of his mum's best cooking and watch some seasonal TV. He made sure he caught up with his friends – they told him that despite his new-found fame he hadn't changed a bit – and he spent a day with his friend and former White Eskimo bandmate Haydn in Manchester, where lots of people stopped him in the street to congratulate him.

On Christmas Eve he called Louis to wish him a happy birthday; he said he missed the others quite a lot during this period and he spoke to Louis on the phone a few times and texted Liam, Zayn and Niall. He did a Twitcam of himself in his bedroom, dressed in a red Santa hat. The video made its way on to the Internet and in it he showed us his present for Louis, which he said he wrapped himself. He'd watched TV and listened to Rihanna. He answered a call from his friend Haydn and said he was 'chuffed' that Matt landed the No. 1 spot with his *X Factor* winner's song. He added that he 'wasn't impressed' after his neighbour woke him up at 9 a.m., playing his bass guitar.

One of the things Harry enjoys doing in his time off is watching films, and over that period he watched many Christmas classics. His favourite flick is *Love Actually*, even though he fibs and says it is *Fight Club* when he is asked because it is manlier. He even recently said he last cried while watching a film and tried to hide his face so no one would see him. He was too ashamed to say what film it was because it wasn't even sad. Instead, he blamed being tired and emotional after travelling for thirty hours straight. Likely story!

Many of his new groupies flocked to his mum's house to see if they could catch him and Harry admitted he felt sorry for them waiting out in the cold. He has always tried to give autographs and speak to his fans whenever he can – he knows that they are the reason for the band's success. He and the other 1D boys have vowed never to take their fans for granted.

He told radio station The End: 'It's all about the fans. We love having the fans; they're incredible so everything we do is for them.'

Part of the boys' big appeal is that they are so accessible and they are just like the boys that their fans might go to school with. They have always admitted that they would date a fan and Harry says that he has snogged 'maybe two' of their followers.

He saw in the end of 2010 with his mates and thought about how his life had changed in just a few short weeks. It was a brilliant end to one of the most important years of his life. But better was yet to come.

2011 kicked off with a series of management meetings and private gigs, including a Sweet 16 party and some lavish batmitzvahs, and then the boys were going to start their lives as proper pop stars. Their first stop? Los Angeles, to start recording tracks for their debut album.

Many of the *X Factor* acts wait a year or more to release their new material but Simon and the Syco team wanted to keep the momentum of the show going and get some music out as quickly as possible.

The trip would be for five days, with two of them spent travelling. When they touched down in sunny LA, they soon forgot about their jetlag and tiredness because they were whisked to the plush W hotel, which is at the foothills of the superstars' capital, Beverly Hills, just moments from Santa Monica beach and Sunset Strip. They attended lots of meetings but also spent some time by the outdoor pool, soaking up the sun in their shorts and t-shirts, and Harry had a massage at the hotel's Bliss Spa because he often gets a bad back. Their rooms were huge and stylish with panoramic views and they were starting to get a taste of what their new lives might be like. They loved the vibe of LA – the people were beautiful, the food was never-ending and the sun shone constantly – it really was like something out of a film. Harry was in his element.

While they were in LA, they met many famous people, including the producer and music man Randy Jackson, whose office was in the building where they had started recording. Harry described him as 'an amazing guy'. The group began laying down tracks with the producer RedOne, the impresario behind the success of Lady Gaga. They were all nervous about working with, and meeting, such important people within the industry but being together made it easier. They would start joking and fooling around, and soon everyone would be at ease.

The boys also had dinner with the producer Max Martin, who has worked with Britney Spears, Katy Perry and Pink, and it seems everyone was starting to see the potential of this new young boyband, particularly Simon, who was growing more excited about the possibilities by the day.

An 'insider' told the *Sunday Mirror*: 'Simon has told industry execs that if One Direction don't have a number one
single and album before the close of 2011, then he'll eat his
hat.'

While they were in LA, they also saw their fellow *X Factor*
finalist Cher, who had flown out a few days earlier to start
working on her music with Cheryl's pal and manager,
will.i.am. The boys met her at a famous shopping spot, the
outdoor mall The Grove, where Harry was seen giving her
a huge hug before heading off to Abercrombie & Fitch,
where he stocked up on his favourite t-shirts. It was good to
see a friendly face.

After a fantastic few days they headed home – and even
though the stay itself was an incredible experience, it was
the moment when they landed back in the UK that would
become the abiding memory from the trip, going down as
something of a legend in the 1D camp.

Simon was correct about the possible success of his boys
judging by their astounding fan base, which was building by
the day. Touching down at Heathrow Airport after their 11-
hour flight, there was only one way out, and this is where
all the paparazzi and fans congregate when they know
someone famous is heading back in to the UK. The boys had
been used to small groups of fans congregating outside the
studio but this crowd was on a completely different scale: it
was immense and like nothing they had seen before.
According to onlookers, the boys went in different directions to try and confuse the photographers but were met by

a wall of hundreds of screaming girls, who leapt on them, trying to take pictures with their cameras and touch them. It was complete chaos: Liam was accidentally knocked around the head and fans grabbed his hat, and the others had their clothing ripped.

It was such a frenzy that their tour manager Paul Higgins, who is with them around the clock, called the police and they had to run as fast as their feet could carry them away from the crowd to the riot van. They were escorted out of the airport with a screech of tyres. Harry found himself really caught up in the moment and admitted that rather than being scared, he was determined to enjoy it. This would be the first of many times when they would need to run for safety from overzealous women. All the boys were breathless and stunned: they were getting this kind of brilliant reaction and they hadn't even released any music yet!

Amusingly, a veteran boybander, Boyzone singer Ronan Keating, was also at the airport. He wrote on Twitter: 'Just landed at Heathrow and when I walked out there were hundreds of screaming fans sadly not for me HaHa. One Direction were on the flight.'

After the scuffle, the boys' management team decided that a huge team of bodyguards would now be needed to protect them. Paul, an Irish security specialist who has worked with Girls Aloud, Boyzone and Westlife, would lead it as their tour manager. All the boys have a brilliant relationship with Paul and cite him as a good friend, saying he is the 'biggest' member of the band. He can often be seen play-fighting with them. True to form, after he got married Harry told him, 'Your wife is hot.' Paul is hugely protective of the group and has been seen getting into scuffles with the paps if they step out of line.

They had a team of people forming around them: Modest! became their management team because they had an exclusive contract with all the acts that made it to the live shows, and they were also looked after by PR firm Hackford Jones, who dealt with requests from journalists eager to speak to them.

During the first week of February the boys started rehearsals for the 37-date *X Factor* tour, which would criss-cross the country, taking in venues including Belfast, Sheffield and Glasgow, before rounding off in Cardiff on 5 April. The lads would be away for a couple of months and they all said they couldn't believe how much stuff they could squeeze into their small suitcases when they had to.

Harry was happy to be reunited with his good friends Aiden and Matt but knew it would be no holiday; they would have work hard.

The whole group went straight into rehearsals at a venue called Light Structures. As well as going over some of the songs they had performed on the show, they were taught more about moving around the stage with ease and speaking to audiences between songs, which felt a bit unnatural when there were only eight crew members listening.

The first night in Birmingham was certainly memorable, with a 12,000-strong crowd cheering them on. The girls went crazy each time Harry's name flashed up on screen and security had to warn the crowd to get back as the audience surged forward in an attempt to get a closer look. Playing massive arenas like this on their first tour was a huge leap for 1D and an opportunity most musicians would not have had for years, but it was a great experience that would set them up for the future.

Unlike the other finalists, 1D were allowed to sing five songs, the same number as the winner, Matt, while the others only had a two-song set. After coming up from lifts under the stage to roars from the crowd, they stole the show with energetic performances of 'Kids in America' and 'Only Girl (In the World)' and they also had a surprise for fans: they had the honour of performing the track they didn't sing on the ITV show – 'Forever Young', their winner's single. They also performed 'Chasing Cars' and 'My Life Would Suck Without You'. They were high on life and Harry felt that he had finally landed where he belonged, describing it as 'incredible'.

They spent a lot of their time travelling but the boys made sure they had fun as they performed to thousands of people every night. They were sharing a dressing room with the other male artists, including their good friends Matt and Aiden, but after the first show Matt asked for one of his own.

He told *OK!* magazine: 'Two shows a day is quite

knackering and full on. I got there and they told me all of the male winners previously had had their own dressing rooms. But I was like "No, I'm the same as them; I don't want my own dressing room." But then one show with One Direction running around screaming their heads off and I said, "Get me my own dressing room."'

There were plenty of pranks, including fruit fights on two occasions which started when Louis threw an apple core in the bin (and then as everyone joined in descended into chaos), while Zayn and Louis had a competition to see who could give each other the deadest arm before they went on stage. On other dates, one of the band members would be charged with inserting random phrases into their performances, like 'shower cubicle', 'winklepickers' or 'Rodney and Del Boy'. One night Louis even managed to do some roly-polys on stage.

The pranks were not just for the rest of 1D: Harry was also happy to terrorise the Brazilian contestant, Wagner. He told 3am.co.uk: 'Wagner fell asleep and I put all the teddies around him and took photos. Picking the best pranks is the hardest bit. Louis Walsh always starts everything. We had a water fight on the bus, that was Louis starting it.'

When Valentine's Day came round, Harry said that the other Louis, Louis Tomlinson, was his choice of Valentine and that the biggest flirt on the tour was Wagner – who bought all the girls a rose. It seems 1D's Louis was getting a name for himself as one of the biggest jokers and Harry complained that he would always wake up from sleeping with two straws up his nostrils because Louis was trying to turn him into a walrus.

Liam said that Louis tried to put the others off their vocals by messing about and one night, in the middle of a live performance, Louis jumped on Harry's back and the pair of them ran in circles around him whilst he tried to not get distracted. Harry simply didn't have time to get homesick: he was having too much fun and didn't want it to stop.

After each show the five-piece would head back to the hotel where they were staying and into a room that had been put aside for them where they could relax and try and come down from the high of playing huge arenas. Their ears would be ringing and it would often be impossible to sleep.

Harry said his best memory was performing in Manchester, where some of his family and friends came along to support him, and that the gig in Dublin was 'crazy'. Harry's mum Anne also went to the gig in Newcastle along with Louis' mum Johanna, who was celebrating her birthday. The two mums have grown really close and keep in touch when the boys are away.

The tour finished with a huge wrap party in a nightclub below a hotel and Harry stayed up until 5 a.m. partying alongside the rest of the artists and the hardworking crew and management teams. They were exhausted but luckily they had the day off to rest. The boys' diary was filling fast and days off would become as precious as gold dust.

Around this time the boys released their first official book, *Forever Young*, and they did a number of signings at WH-Smiths in Lakeside, Liverpool and Westfield and Selfridges in Manchester, where many fans had queued through the night to get near them. Harry hugged the lucky few, signed copies and posed for pictures. He said he was given a lot of turtles at the signings after he once said he liked them. He was surprised that people listened to every small thing he mentioned.

During one signing he showed off his new bromance with a t-shirt which read 'Harry hearts Louis'! In Manchester, he got the most screams – which was fast becoming the case everywhere – and also brought out another message t-shirt, stating the rather obvious 'Tofu Guys Don't Eat Meat'. *Forever Young* soon shot to the top of the *Sunday Times* bestseller list, a huge achievement, which Harry said was 'pretty unbelievable'.

Harry was then allowed some proper time off – it would be his last holiday for a while – and he and Louis each took a friend to Courchevel in the Alps in France, where they went skiing. Harry had never skied before and was eager to learn. Harry took his mate Johnny and Louis took his best friend, Stan.

The boys were closer than ever. Louis' mum Johanna commented: 'I really like Harry. I liked him from the first day I met him. They definitely do have a really strong bond. It's not a fabricated thing; it's not contrived. It's not something they thought they'd do to see if they could get any mileage out of it. They're like brothers. They genuinely respect and love each other.'

It was good for them to have a well-earned break and Louis revealed that while they might have a huge following not everyone abroad knew who they were – the pair were left red-faced after some fellow holidaymakers asked for a picture.

'One time Harry and I were skiing together when a girl and a guy came up to us with a camera,' he told *Seventeen* magazine. 'We assumed they were going to ask us for a photo so we stood there with our arms around each other posing. They said, "No we want you to take a photo of us! It was embarrassing."'

Then it was back home for more work and a number of television appearances, including *The Alan Titchmarsh Show*. Harry even charmed Alan, saying he used to watch his show *Ground Force* when he was little, and would wheel a wheelbarrow around. He says he will always remember the occasion, as it was their first proper TV interview after they were signed. He still couldn't believe that everyone wanted to know every small thing about him but he was happy to talk and very relaxed about it all.

It wasn't just the TV producers who were after Harry and co. The big brands were cottoning on to their appeal to the teen market and the boys won their first big endorsement deal for the Nintendo brand Pokémon. It wasn't hard work for them either: their television commercial for the brand showed them clowning around and they filmed a series of video diaries while they were on the *X Factor* tour, which were similarly fun. Harry said that the Pokémon characters are like pets that you look after and jested: 'I'm good friends with my Pokémon. I bring them up as my crew.' One of the diaries showed him thinking he could fly and launching himself from a chair to the floor.

However, while they were having lots of fun, what the boys really wanted was the chance to make music properly. Their first decision? Choosing a debut single.

CHAPTER FIVE

'We worked really hard on the first album to find the right songs'

On the X *Factor* tour Harry and the other boys had started messing around with tunes and lyrics, deciding what sort of direction they wanted their music to take, and they couldn't wait to begin properly recording their debut album.

They started work at the Cosmos and Kinglet Studios in Stockholm and then went back to the studio in the UK, a period which they described as 'really intense' as they laid down vocals and finely tuned their first releases. They also returned to the bright lights of LA for another three weeks as they prepared to bring out their first single and album.

Harry said: 'We worked really hard on the first album to find the right songs. They needed to be perfect. We wanted our first single to be a big summer song. For instance when the Black Eyed Peas single "I Gotta Feeling" came out in 2009 it was the song of the summer. When everyone heard it, it reminded them of all the good times they'd had. We wanted our first single to be like that and be the song that everyone would remember.' He also explained that they wanted a song that people 'didn't expect'.

The boys worked with a number of big producers including Steve Robson, Rami Yacoub, Carl Falk and Savan Kotecha. Savan, who worked with the boys on *The X Factor* and has penned tracks for Britney Spears, Leona Lewis, Usher and JLS, told *Digital Spy*: 'I've been in the early stages of helping to develop a few things for them . . . For them it's just going to be experimenting with a few things – they're going to be fine. They've got some really good songs. The stuff I've heard has been really catchy and everyone loves the guys, so it's just about capturing that in the music, which I think is what they're going to be doing.'

Syco were really excited about the forthcoming releases and the boys spent a few weeks out of the limelight as they worked at it, taking time to decide on their lead single. They chose their song, an uplifting pop-rock anthem called 'What Makes You Beautiful'. There was a lot of expectation and the immense pressure that goes with that but the boys were confident that it was the perfect choice.

Written by Rami, Carl and Savan, the single has a fun, uptempo feel to it, and begins with a guitar riff, which many said sounded like the famous *Grease* track 'Summer Nights'. Liam sings the first verse, a tried and tested method the boys

Where it all began.
The newly formed
One Direction head
to rehearsals for the
X Factor live shows

© Press Association Images

The 1D boys are massive fans of their
onesies and sparked a fashion trend when
they were snapped wearing them!

© Rex Features

It was love at first sight for
'Larry Stylinson'

© Rex Features

The boys and 'Uncle Simon' at the *X Factor* final press conference
© Getty Images

Fans wait eagerly outside Harry's home for him to arrive for a flying visit
© Rex Features

Harry and his BFF Nick
'Grimmy' Grimshaw
© Rex Features

The boys pose
with their BRIT
Award – Harry
said he planned
to put his in his
loo at home!
© Rex Features

Harry gets the crowds going
during NBC's *Today* show at
Rockefeller Plaza. Five million
people tuned in to watch 1D's
performance
© Rex Features

Harry sets his sights on Kim Kardashian with this cheeky message
© Rex Features

Stripping off in Sydney Harbour and displaying his four nipples!
© Rex Features

Harry gives model Emma Ostilly a goodnight kiss
© Rex Features

The boys perform 'What Makes You Beautiful' during the London Olympics closing ceremony, in front of an audience of billions. Harry said the experience 'can't be topped'
© Rex Features

Katy Perry steals a kiss at the
MTV Video Music Awards
© Rex Features

Harry takes
his seat in the
exclusive front
row during
Burberry's
London Fashion
Week show
© Rex Features

The boys'
worldwide
takeover
continues as
they star on the
US *X Factor*
© Rex Features

During a soulful performance of
'Little Things' on the US *X Factor*
© Getty Images

Harry shows off his cheeky
dimples on the *Today* show
© Getty Images

The new hot couple
'Haylor' head out of their
hotel in New York on a
romantic date
© Rex Features

1D wow the enormous crowd at New York's iconic Madison Square Garden

A huge fan of body art, Harry shows off his latest inkings while on holiday in the Caribbean

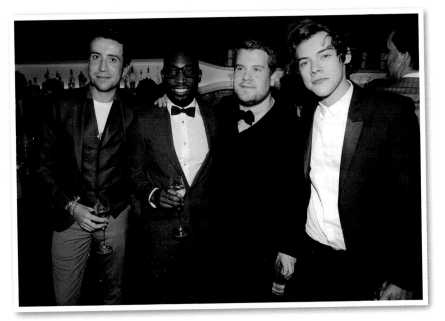

Harry poses with his celebrity mates Grimmy, James Corden and Tinie Tempah at a private party celebrating a week of men's London fashion events

© Rex Features

Their global domination continues as One Direction mania hits Japan in January 2013

© Rex Features

had used in the *X Factor* shows, and Harry's soulful voice then comes in during the bridge, where they all join together for the anthemic chorus. Zayn takes on the second verse with a harder edge to his voice, then Harry's dreamy vocals bridge back to the chorus. In the middle of the song Harry performs an a cappella interlude before the chorus comes crashing in once again. Harry closes the song with the words, 'That's what makes you beautiful.' It was 3 minutes 18 seconds of pop perfection and had fans young and old dancing around their front rooms, singing along in the car and bopping in the school playground.

It received its first airplay on Scott Mills' Radio 1 show on 10 August, with Harry announcing to MTV: 'We're so excited to get the single finally out there. I think for us we wanted to release something that wasn't cheesy but was fun. It kind of represented us. I think it took us a while to find it but I think we found the right song.'

As they prepared for the world exclusive, the boys had a group hug and then did a celebratory dance as it played across the airwaves. They didn't know how the single would be received and waited anxiously as the fans and critics had their say but they needn't have worried: the country went wild for it! Three weeks ahead of its official release, it was confirmed that a record had already been broken when Simon Cowell's right-hand man Sonny Takhar announced that they had achieved the highest ever amount of pre-orders for any Sony Music act. And he described the boyband's upcoming debut album as one of the best pop records to be made by the label, which is home to acts like Michael Jackson, Beyoncé and Christina Aguilera.

The critics also loved it. *Digital Spy*'s Robert Copsey gave it four out of five stars and described it as a cross between McFly and Pink, labelling it 'adorable' and 'likely to cause a stir amongst your mates'. BBC's *Newsround* also gave it four out of five and called it 'fun, upbeat and incredibly catchy'. Even music bible *NME* stated that it was 'exuberant with a catchy "oh na na" middle eight'.

The video, which was filmed over two days in July, saw the lads driving along a highway in a camper van before parking up by the shoreline on a beach in Malibu, California. Directed by photographer and cinematographer John Urbano, the group stroll around the beach and dance in the white surf, singing 'What Makes You Beautiful', before a few young girls join them for a beach party as the sun sets in the distance. During Harry's a cappella notes towards the end of the song, he cosies up with a lucky brunette model, called Madison McMillin, who looks very happy with the set-up – and Harry is said to have had a bit of a crush on her when they were filming.

They started releasing teaser clips of the video on the band's official website – something they would continue to do with each new single – before releasing the full version on YouTube. It has now had over 170 million views.

When 1D later appeared on the *Alan Carr: Chatty Man* show, Alan asked Harry if he got close to any of the girls whilst filming and Harry replied: 'The girls were lovely in the video.' Then, as if he wasn't embarrassed enough, Alan put up a photo of Madison and asked: 'So Harry. What happened between you and Madison? Did you take a trip down Madison Avenue?' The other boys fell about laughing.

The question Harry was now being asked constantly was: what makes a girl beautiful? Everyone wanted to get his attention and thought they were in with a chance of being his girlfriend, a fact Harry found both flattering and unexpected.

Harry says he likes girls who play hard to get. In an interview with *Top of the Pops* magazine, he added: 'The fun part is the chase, so if you speak to me, play a bit hard to get. I think it's attractive when someone turns you down. You don't want someone to say yes straight away, do you?'

He has said that he wants someone loyal and with a good sense of humour, who he can introduce to his parents, and someone 'he could call in the middle of the night and just talk to'. He also told *Heat* magazine that he prefers 'curvy' girls as there is 'more to grab on to', and when he was asked if he likes boobs, legs or bums, he replied: 'All of them. But I'm more into legs and bums.'

A few days before the single release, the band performed the track live for the first time on TV show *Red or Black?* back on ITV. It was a massive, energetic performance and there was loads of expectation. Sadly for him, Harry's nerves were all too visible again – he was breathless after jumping up and down on stage and his hands were shaking. He showed how stressed he was with a slightly petrified look on his face and as he sang his a cappella lines, he seemed to lose his voice towards the end. As he finished, he breathed a sigh of relief and Niall patted his shoulder to try and give him a reassuring sign that he had done OK, but he knew it wasn't his best and was hugely disappointed in himself. The group then burst into the loud and bouncy chorus.

Harry said it was a 'massive wake-up call' and that it was his 'low point'. After they went backstage, they were congratulated by everyone and hugged each other but Harry was gutted and really took his feelings to heart. He felt like he had let the rest of the group down and wished he could do it again and show how much better he could do. While the other boys celebrated their first live performance as a signed act, Harry was quiet and subdued and texted his mum and friends, looking for reassurance. Showing his relative naivety, he then went straight online and searched 'Harry's shit' to see what people were saying about him. He found loads of bad comments about his performance.

In the ITV2 show *One Direction: A Year in the Making*, Harry is seen crying to the camera: 'I read a massive list of these comments. You read through, for example your Twitter feed. If there is three people saying you're amazing you don't think why are they saying I'm amazing, they say I'm amazing 'cos they're a fan. But if there is one saying they hate me, why do they hate me? What have I done? I can take criticism. I can definitely take criticism but it is just like a "I don't like you." I want to know why people don't like me.'

When the show aired and Harry's true feelings about that night emerged, #poorharry started trending on Twitter. He was clearly touched and wrote: 'Hope everyone enjoyed the documentary! Thank you all so much for giving us this incredible opportunity . . . we love you. .xx'

He knew he would have to toughen up, as not everyone would like him all the time, but it was hard. Harry really cared what people thought. He would soon have to learn to ignore the negative comments on Twitter.

But regardless of this small mishap, the boys went on a promotional tour of lots of radio stations to do interviews to publicise the single and they always sang live, something many acts will not do, while Niall strummed along on the guitar. They were natural, funny and great singers and they went down a storm wherever they went.

On the day of release – 11 September – the boys took a private helicopter and went from Glasgow to London to Manchester, where they were greeted by hundreds of fans who had queued to see them. It seemed like they were having exciting new experiences every day and travelling by helicopter was a fantastic event. They relaxed in sumptuous leather seats between stops and made sure they had a change of clothes between each one, too. They were never demanding but their every whim was catered for. There was food and drink on tap and computer games to help them relax. It was teenage-boy heaven.

Fans camped outside venues where the boys were heading with the hope of catching a glimpse of their favourite member as the group kept to their strict timetable, seeing as many fans as they could before dashing back to the helicopter for their next stop.

Their promotional tour continued and on one occasion when they were promoting the single on 98FM station in Dublin, the boys sent a load of Domino's pizzas out to the girls in case they were hungry because many of them had been queuing since 5 a.m.

Their fan base clearly adored 'What Makes You Beautiful' and Harry also teased the girls by getting them excited about the rest of the album. He said: 'It's crazy but we're really enjoying ourselves. We have a whole album and we are really pleased with it.' Everyone was desperate to hear it.

Not only were they swarmed by girls everywhere they turned, it seems many started to use novel ways to try and get their attention, even throwing sanitary towels with their Twitter names written on them, along with tampons. They often wanted the boys to sign different body parts including their big toes and their boobs.

Harry told *Fabulous* magazine: 'I was in the park the other day and a woman ran up to me and asked for my autograph. She handed me a pen and I asked her if she had a piece of paper. She just looked at me and got out her boobs!' This would be the start of many weird and wonderful ways fans tried to get handsome Harry's attention as the weeks went past.

On the Sunday after release the boys were back at Radio 1

with Reggie Yates – and they cheered when they found out they had landed the No. 1 slot, taking the baton from Pixie Lott. Another record had been broken: the song had racked up the highest first-week sales of any UK single released in 2011. Over a thousand people had turned up at the studio in Maida Vale to see them arrive at the chart show, so BBC bosses were forced to cancel and film them in a 'secret location' instead. It was always 'amazing' – they didn't know how else to describe what they were going through.

Simon was over the moon with the group's success and made sure he spoiled his new protégés. He took them and another of his acts, Leona Lewis, to The Savoy hotel for a fundraising dinner for the Katie Piper Foundation, of which he is a patron. Harry looked extremely suave in his black suit and bow tie, smiling with his perfect white teeth on the red carpet, proving why he was starting to earn his reputation as a heartbreaker. Even though the group joked that Simon Cowell was paying them 'in sweets', Harry still bid £7000 for two Grand Prix tickets. He also stole Niall's bidding card and put an £8000 bid on a beauty school workshop without his bandmate knowing. Luckily for him, he was outbid!

A couple of days later, they were at the *GQ* Men of the Year awards at London's Royal Opera House in Covent Garden, along with the great and good of showbiz including Emma Watson, Kelly Brook, Kylie Minogue and The Saturdays. Harry was wearing a gorgeous Lanvin suit and another bow tie, which seemed to be growing a fan club of its own, with competitions popping up on websites and in magazines to win one!

It was events such as these that made Harry realise how far he had come, although it wasn't just the gorgeous ladies he was excited about meeting, he was bumping into acting legends. He said his highlight was seeing Bill Nighy, who looked 'sick'. He sat on a table with Nick Grimshaw and James Corden and the men dished out advice to 1D on the perils of fame.

During September the group helped Niall celebrate his eighteenth birthday at G-A-Y, where he was presented with a giant cake on stage. Even though they were getting older, the boys showed that they were still as immature as ever and duly had a huge cake fight on stage, chucking great chunks of sponge and icing at each other and into the happy crowd.

Earlier in the night, during their performance of 'What Makes You Beautiful', Harry was left embarrassed when he tripped over with excitement. Radio 1 DJ Greg James wrote on Twitter afterwards: 'Oh @Harry_Styles – that was a text-book fall. 10/10. Bravo.' Harry shrugged off the fall, replying: 'Thank you mate! I tried to style it out . . . it just, didn't work. Haha!'

A few weeks later the band announced their first proper tour, with a string of dates across the UK, starting that December. When the 21 dates went on sale, the thousands of tickets were sold out within a few minutes – the sort of demand associated with A-list stars like Justin Bieber and the

Rolling Stones. Just hours later ticket touts were trying to sell them for as much as £200 a pair.

They didn't have time to think too hard about this incredible achievement as they were so busy starting to plan the huge show, sitting down with the producers and team involved in bringing it to life and going through the set list, themes and what would happen in each song.

Harry told *First News*: 'We always sit and talk about ideas and have a meeting to talk about what we can do and what we want to do. We talked a lot about what we want to get from the tour and what songs we want to do. We're really involved, which means it'll be a really personal show.'

Their success wasn't just going to be in the UK: news of 1D was spreading like wildfire to Europe and they went on a short tour called Bring 1D To Me, visiting four countries in four days. Life was getting so busy for the boys they often didn't know where they would be each day or what they would be doing; they just relied on the team of people who were managing them to guide them.

They started in sunny Stockholm, where they did an interview and performance of 'What Makes You Beautiful' at the Café Opera. As the crowd of fans, dubbed Directioners, let out high-pitched screams, Harry took centre stage and said, 'This is amazing!' To everyone's elation, he also practised his Swedish, saying a few choice phrases like 'I love you', and the girls went wild.

During a group interview he was asked some random questions and he said that if he wasn't a pop star, he'd like to be a physiotherapist. When he was asked if he could have a superpower what would it be, he replied time travel! But as he spoke, girls at the front were being crushed because there was so much jostling, and they had to urge the crowd to move back. There were banners and gifts for the boys – one girl made super-cute figurines of each of them out of icing. And Louis revealed that another girl even hid in a bin in an attempt to get close to them!

Everywhere they went Harry was bombarded with proposals of marriage – but he doesn't mind them. 'It's not embarrassing at all,' he told *Top of the Pops* magazine. 'I quite like it! I think it's really flattering and quite cute most of the time.'

From Sweden, they travelled to Milan in Italy, where a crowd of 3000 had turned out. As they arrived the girls burst into the chorus of 'What Makes You Beautiful'. From here they travelled to Munich. Once again they did some interviews and Harry revealed he could also speak a bit of German and that he thinks 'Emma Watson is hot' – and the boys did another acoustic performance, much to the delight of their new army of followers.

Their final stop was Amsterdam, where they sang at the Hotel Arena. Along with the performance came more foreign words spoken by Harry during the group interview – cue more squeals – and the admission that if he was an animal he would like to be a cat!

The tour showed the phenomenal power of social media. Even though the boys had yet to release 'What Makes You

Beautiful' in these countries, due to the power of YouTube, Twitter, Facebook and Tumblr and the marketing campaign, girls were everywhere they went, trying to catch the boys' attention and creating hysteria. Louis said: 'It just shows how powerful the Internet is. . . . That's basically what spread the word.' Niall added: 'If you ask our fans where they found out about us it's always Twitter, YouTube, Tumblr, Facebook: it's the most powerful thing we have.'

And Harry explained to the *Guardian* that rather than out-sourcing their Twitter feed to a record company employee like many other celebrities do because they don't have time, the boys run their own in order to give fans the personal touch.

'It's really important that we connect directly with our fans through the likes of Twitter so they can get to know us. There'd be no point someone in the office doing it because that would defeat the object. We kept in contact with them and gave them something to look forward to. If it wasn't us on the thing, the fans wouldn't know us.'

Talking to *Popdirt*, he explained: 'I think it adds pressure. Every time you go to tweet, you have to think a lot of people are gonna see this. I did tweet a while ago that I really fancy a donut and I did get a few actually.'

All the boys are always on Twitter, talking to their fans every day about their work alongside the normal stuff that they are up to.

The 1D fans are so hardcore that they started to create their own language, with words including 'extraordinharry', used for describing a picture of Harry that they can't find the words for; 'Harry's hipsters' for those who are fans of Harry before being supporters of the band; and 'HLH', an acronym for 'hair like Harry'.

There was no relaxing when they got back to the UK after their tour in Europe. They appeared at the BBC Radio 1 Teen Awards at Wembley Arena, where Harry performed along with the boys to a very noisy crowd. Liam said: 'We had our ear pieces in but it was so so loud. We just thought "Woah".' Afterwards, the boys larked around on stage with host Nick Grimshaw.

Nick, a radio and TV presenter, would become a good friend to Harry. Brought up in Oldham in Manchester, he joined Radio 1 in September 2007, presenting the youth strand *Switch*. Following a stint fronting the *Breakfast Show*, he then took over the 10 p.m.-to-midnight slot. His TV work included hosting Channel 4's *Freshly Squeezed* with Alexa Chung and Jameela Jamil. He and Harry have a very similar sense of humour.

1D's first album *Up All Night* was released on 18 November and includes songs written by Ed Sheeran, Kelly Clarkson and McFly's Tom Fletcher. Filled to the brim with anthemic pop-rock hits, bouncy power pop and soulful ballads, it became the UK's fastest-selling debut album of 2011.

Up All Night features thirteen tracks and the first song on the album is 'What Makes You Beautiful', which was obviously their big, breakthrough single. 'Gotta Be You' is the second-listed track on the album and was also the boys' second released single. Track number three, 'One Thing', is another pop-rock number, with the same writers and production team as 'What Makes You Beautiful'. Track number four, 'More Than This', is a mature and classic ballad and Harry's favourite song from the album. The fifth track on the album, 'Up All Night', namechecks Katy Perry and is catchy and has more of a rock sound, while 'I Wish', number six, is slightly more mid-tempo.

'Tell Me A Lie', the next song, was originally intended for Kelly Clarkson, who co-wrote it. She told Capital FM: 'It's a really cute song, I love it. I loved that they liked it. They sound really great on it. I already have it – I'm so VIP with my copy on my computer! It does sound really good.'

Harry and the boys had a hand in writing number eight, 'Taken', where Harry's vocals feature heavily. McFly star Tom Fletcher co-wrote track number nine, 'I Want', with the boys. He later reminisced about their days in the studio, telling the Press Association: 'They're exactly like we were when we started. The first time I was in the studio with them, I suddenly felt really old because they have all this lingo that I don't even know any more and I'm well past it now.'

The tenth track is called 'Everything About You' and is another uptempo electropop number and eleven, 'Same Mistakes', is a slower tempo song. The final two tracks are 'Save You Tonight' and 'Stole My Heart', both energetic pop songs. The album was also released as a limited edition yearbook compilation, which included two bonus tracks, 'Stand

Up' and 'Moments', a pop ballad which was written by Ed Sheeran.

Harry had the most solo time on the album at around seven minutes, with Liam coming second with six minutes.

It debuted at No. 2 in the UK charts and became the fastest-selling debut album on the UK Albums Chart of 2011.

The album was met with mixed reviews: *Cosmopolitan* magazine said it was full of 'toe-tappers that are just impossible to dislike' and *PopMatters* said it was a 'well-crafted slice of pop you can pop bubbles to'. *The Sun*'s Gordon Smart added: 'Up All Night will be lapped up by their young fan base.' However, *The Independent* gave it just two out of five stars, labelling it 'offensive daytime radio pop', and *Rolling Stone* called them 'one dimensional'.

The boys didn't take the negative comments too much to heart – the huge sales spoke for themselves.

One of the album's slower numbers, 'Gotta Be You', was released as a single in the same month. Harry wrote on Twitter: 'I think it's just swell.' More emotive and thoughtful than their first offering, it was written by August Rigo and Steve Mac, who has produced more than twenty-three No. 1 singles in the UK.

The video, which was filmed at Lake Placid, New York, saw Harry, wrapped in a cosy cream scarf and orange jumper and coat, walking through a college campus singing, Louis driving a Mini, and Zayn on a train. They meet with Niall and Liam by a cabin in a forest where they sit around an open fire with some pretty girls and fireworks burst into the sky.

The shooting of the video was apparently hit by all sorts of problems. Zayn reportedly crashed his moped into a wall while Louis burned out the cooling system on the Mini. Liam also said they were worried they might be attacked by crocodiles after they went kayaking and Niall toppled them over.

The single was well reviewed by the critics again: *Digital Spy* gave it four out of five stars, while *Cosmopolitan* magazine said it 'blew them away'. However, it didn't do quite as well as 'What Makes You Beautiful', only reaching No. 3 in the UK charts behind Rihanna's 'We Found Love' and Flo Rida's 'Good Feeling'.

Nonetheless, the boys were certainly on a roll and had commitments almost every day, with a series of promotional performances at Children in Need 2011 and Capital FM's Jingle Bell Ball at The O2 arena, along with Jessie J, JLS, The Saturdays, Ed Sheeran, Emeli Sandé and Wretch 32. The five-piece sang 'Gotta Be You', 'What Makes You Beautiful' and 'One Thing'.

Indulging in a slightly random conversation backstage with presenter Roberto, Harry said he was getting into the Christmas spirit by eating mince pies – and he said he wouldn't change anything about the previous year. Talking about his favourite sandwich he said it was ham, cheese and Branston pickle.

The awards were rolling in: they scooped Best Group, Best Breakthrough and Best Video at the 4Music Video

Honours. In their video message, Harry said: 'It just shows how dedicated our fans are that so many went out to vote for us, so thank you very much.'

It seemed that 1D could do no wrong as far as their devoted fans were concerned.

CHAPTER SIX

'To Flackster! Never too old . . .
Lets make it happen!!'

A couple of months earlier, Harry and the gang had gone partying at the exclusive W Hotel in Leicester Square after one of the *X Factor* finals and it was here that Harry famously hooked up with Caroline Flack, who he had spoken about having a long-term crush on. Harry had talked about how he fancied her, describing her as 'very, very beautiful – very pretty' and 'gorgeous', saying he hoped they would spend some proper time together when the boys went on the show. She is known for her fun sense of humour, charm and girl-next-door looks and is exactly the type Harry would go for.

The host of the *X Factor* spin-off show, *The Xtra Factor*, Caroline, who was thirty-one at the time, has had a diverse TV career. She got her break into TV in 2002 on the sketch show *Bo' Selecta!* on Channel 4 and then presented *The Games: Live At Trackside* and *When Games Attack*. She moved to the BBC a year later to present *TMi* and *Escape from Scorpion Island* on CBBC. She followed this with a stint on *Big Brother's Big Mouth* before moving to present *Gladiators* alongside Ian Wright on Sky1. She then started on *I'm a Celebrity . . . Get Me Out of Here! Now!* on ITV2 and fronted the jungle survival spin-off for two years.

Caroline's romantic antics were the subject of much scrutiny and she kicked up a media storm when she was rumoured to be dating Prince Harry – five years her junior – after they were introduced by mutual friends at a poker tournament in April 2009. They were said to have hit it off instantly and she even gave him the moniker 'jam' because 'he had jam-coloured hair and was sweet'. Apparently they exchanged a number of flirty messages and Caroline posted on her Facebook wall 'Caroline loves jam . . . x'.

Just a couple of weeks later in June, Harry reportedly dumped her after pining for his long-term girlfriend, Chelsy Davy. But Caroline later denied they were ever a couple, telling the *Daily Mail*: 'I met him a few times and we got on fine but we were never a couple.' She also denied that 'jam' referred to him – it was a nickname for one of her closest friends.

Prior to her encounter with Prince Harry, she had dated Dave 'Danger' Healy for three years. He was a former drummer in rock band, The Holloways, who she said was the love of her life.

As Harry and Caroline partied the night away with the cast and crew of the ITV show, the pair were talking for some time before Harry apparently made a move on Caroline and kissed her. An onlooker told the *Daily Mirror*: 'They had a big passionate snog and it caused mild hysterics with the group of people they were with. They looked really into each other and left in a cab together, eventually going their separate ways – much to the amusement of the group.'

The couple gave the game away after they both complained about feeling ill on their Twitter pages the next day – prompting speculation that they had caught the same bug. Following the encounter, Harry wrote on Twitter: 'Sometimes things happen and you suddenly get a whole new outlook on life.' Caroline then added: 'Woke up with the sorest throat and huge glands,' and then referencing her kiss with Harry, added: 'Harry Styles, Lou Teasdale, Tom Atkin, Valerie Teasdale, we ate the same stew ... People will talk. :).'

According to insiders Caroline found Harry fun, charismatic and charming and they got on brilliantly, but the kiss was a one-off and she wasn't interested in pursuing a relationship, mainly because of the large age gap.

But perhaps her reluctance made Harry keener on her and when 1D were set to perform their new single 'Gotta Be You' on *The X Factor* just less than a month later in November, he tweeted her prior to the performance. 'I hope @carolineflack1 likes my shoes today ...' he wrote, to which she replied: '@Harry_Styles I'm worried that I won't, could be awkward . . .'.

The performance saw 1D styled to perfection in coordinating colours of blue, white, grey, maroon and bright red. Harry was wearing maroon skinny jeans, a crisp white t-shirt and blue jacket. They couldn't believe a year had gone past since they had last stood on that very stage. It seemed quite amazing that just twelve months earlier they were nervously awaiting their fate to see if they would stay in the competition.

Harry told Dermot O'Leary: 'This studio is amazing. It's amazing to be back today and see the crew.' And afterwards he said on Twitter: 'performing on x factor . . .was such a humbling experience. Reminded us all how lucky we are :) x'.

However, Caroline and Harry's blossoming romance was still at the forefront of everyone's thoughts. During *The Xtra Factor*, Louis Walsh also poked fun at Caroline, saying to fellow judge Gary Barlow: 'By the way Gary – somebody's made a big effort today for some reason. Caroline is looking really well, she's trying to impress somebody tonight. I don't know who it is.'

Louis also retweeted a message from a fan, saying: 'Go on, make it awkward between Harry and Caroline tonight :)' And Louis was quick to answer Caroline's co-host Olly Murs' question to Harry asking him which *X Factor* girl Harry fancied the most, by shouting 'Caroline!'

Harry admitted that he had been waiting for someone to

bring it up and the audience cheered loudly. The young star added fuel to the fire when he was asked which of this year's girls he fancied and he said they were a bit young for him – even though many were his age.

Harry wasn't the first member of 1D to date an older woman. Zayn had hooked up with fellow finalist Rebecca Ferguson earlier in the year for four months, splitting in July 2011. Rebecca was six years Zayn's senior and also mum to two young children. She blamed 1D's management, saying that she was bad for their image, and also revealed that she went through a 'hard time'. Zayn later said that the relationship was the 'wrong' decision and that it ended badly.

After the show Caroline, who was wearing a black dress, woollen coat and had bare legs, was seen hugging Niall as the group left the studios. Harry was looking over but the pair studiously avoided catching each other's eye. Hordes of fans queued to try and get a glimpse of them, sticking mobile phones under the gate.

A relationship was almost certainly on the cards and the following Tuesday night the pair were spotted having dinner together at Asia de Cuba at the swanky St Martin's Lane hotel in London, which is a favourite with celebrities, after attending a showbiz party together. They were eating their meal with two other friends and apparently they didn't care who saw them. They appeared smitten and onlookers said they 'only had eyes for each other'. At 11 p.m., they sped off in a chauffeur-driven car together and, again, they didn't seem worried if they were spotted.

Harry was determined to win Caroline over and amusingly posted a photo of himself on Twitter, holding a sign which said: 'To Flackster! Never too old ... Lets make it happen!! Lots of Love Harry S.'

It seemed things were hotting up – and Louis said that Harry thought he had found 'the one' in Caroline – but since rumours of their first kiss, they were both terrified by the response from fans.

As momentum gathered, 1D's fans appeared to be divided over what was soon coined 'Harrygate'. Many supported the couple but scarily Caroline had been receiving abuse from some of Harry's fans and even had death threats from some trolls.

One angry fan wrote: 'If Caroline Flack flirts with my boyfriend I will personally hunt her down and shoot her.' Another angry Tweeter posted: 'I want to kill you Caroline Flack, Harry is mine B***h,' while one said she 'should be having kids, not dating them'. One branded her a 'saggy old woman' and another 'a paedophile', because of the age difference between the couple. Some simply penned: 'DIE!'

Caroline was apparently horrified by what she had been sent and was forced to write on Twitter: 'Hi One Direction fans! To clarify. I'm close friends with harry ... He's one of the nicest people I know ... I don't deserve death threats. :) x.'

Harry was quick to try and calm her down, calling her to try and reassure her that it would blow over. He also tried to placate his fans but still didn't deny he and Caroline were an item, instead saying that they were friends and they would see what happened. He wanted to date her even if his fans didn't like it.

Rather than put an end to the debate, Caroline's message appeared to do the opposite. Many girls continued to bombard her with nasty comments while others tweeted her words of support. One wrote: 'Can't believe that @carolineflack1 is getting death threats :o as much as I love @onedirection I wouldn't threaten to kill someone.'

Caroline's journalist friend Dawn Porter was also on hand to offer support. She wrote: 'To anyone who sent @carolineflack1 nasty or aggressive messages yesterday, I would like to say this, you are repulsive. Chin up girl x.'

And her *Xtra Factor* co-host Olly tried to defend her, saying what she did was her own business, but the cougar debate continued to rage. Many speculated that the relationship was just casual and it is claimed that Harry was seen swapping numbers with 2011 *X Factor* star, Amelia Lily.

In an attempt to show that the relationship wasn't 'exclusive', Louis told *The Sun*: 'The worst thing about living with Harry is the constant stream of women he is getting through the door. It's relentless.'

However, in a revealing interview with *Now* magazine, Caroline was unrepentant and said: 'I feel like I shouldn't have to worry about what I do. But it's a social thing that people aren't accepting of big age gaps.' Defending the fifteen years between them, she added: 'I keep thinking, "What have I done wrong?" But I haven't done anything wrong. What's hard for me to get my head around is people saying it's disgusting. I don't think it is.'

She did say she was trying to brush it off and not take all the comments to heart and also added that Harry had told her to ignore Twitter, saying he was 'mature' about it. He had clearly learnt the hard way that it was best to ignore the horrible comments some people wrote.

Interestingly, Caroline had still failed to deny they were a couple, as had Harry, who continued to say she was a 'lovely woman' and 'hot'. It was clear he really, really liked her.

Meanwhile the boys brought London's West End to a standstill while they filmed the video for their third single, 'One Thing'. They started their day in Battersea Park, where they unleashed their childish side bouncing on space hoppers, kicking toy footballs and doing wheelies on bikes. They then boarded a traditional, open-top red bus to Trafalgar Square and Harry Tweeted: 'Trafalgar Square . . . Let's Do It!'

As they were driven through London, more and more girls turned out to see them, running past the Lyceum Theatre after them. When they waved, many Directioners broke down in floods of tears with the emotion of it all.

The boys then hopped off the bus in the main square, where they busked and everyone joined in. The director of the video, Declan Whitebloom, said they were hoping for a Monkees or Beatles-style result, to create some 'magic'. For some lucky fans, the long wait to see them was worth it: the boys asked some of the girls to star in the video alongside them. All was well with Harry's fans once more. It was a long day and Harry was filmed behind the scenes having a quick nap before they went to Covent Garden for the final wrap.

The single was released on 13 February 2012, with the video premiering a month before on the boy's official website. Syco described the song as an 'epic pop smash-in-waiting, featuring soaring vocal harmonies, powerhouse guitar riffs and an anthemic chorus that refuses to leave your head.' Again the critics' responses were good with *Digital Spy* labelling it 'arena-ready', while *Billboard* said it was 'perfectly-executed pop-rock'.

Some fans even released a hilarious spoof video of babies playing the boys on YouTube, which has had over 2.5 million hits.

It was pictures at the start of December that got everyone talking about Harry and Caroline once again. Harry was seen leaving Caroline's flat in Muswell Hill at 9.30 a.m. carrying an overnight bag – and his famous mop of curly hair was looking particularly scruffy. Caroline herself appeared two hours later dressed in skinny jeans and hiding behind designer sunglasses. *The Sun* reported that Harry had arrived late the previous evening and Caroline had stocked up on food and wine for their romantic night in together.

The nation couldn't get enough of their romance and there was no avoiding questions about it. When Caroline appeared on *Daybreak* alongside Olly Murs, the pro-gramme's host Kate Garraway asked if she was in love and she laughed off the question saying: 'He's a lot younger than me, which some people say is strange.' But she was more defiant, adding that she really liked him and they had fun together. She then quickly returned to the safer subjects of *The X Factor* and girl group Little Mix.

To many fans the new romance just made them crazier about Harry and a huge crowd were left disappointed during the Christmas lights switch-on in Knutsford, which is just a few miles from Harry's native Holmes Chapel. Rumour had spread like wildfire on Twitter that Harry would be there to do the honours but, in the end, Chancellor George Osbourne turned out to flick the festive switch. One girl had appeared with 'I Love Harry' painted on her face and one teen tweeted that she had been expecting the 'teen heartthrob' but instead had got 'The Prince of Darkness'. Unfortunately for his female flock of followers, Harry was miles away back in London rehearsing with his bandmates.

On 9 December Caroline and Harry were seen at a Coldplay gig at The O2 arena. It was their first public date. They were said to have slipped in and out quietly to avoid drawing too much attention. They had a great night watching one of Harry's favourite bands and appeared 'smitten' with one another.

The following evening was the *X Factor* final, where 1D were due to perform, and reports emerged that Harry and Caroline were going to be kept at opposite ends of the studio, with TV bosses concerned about their 'casual mischief'. Bosses supposedly took them to one side and told them in no uncertain terms to stay apart. Presumably they wanted the attention to be on the TV show and the finalists Little Mix, Marcus Collins and Amelia Lily, not the romance going on behind the scenes.

The group performed a rousing mash-up of 'She Makes Me Wanna' and 'What Makes You Beautiful' along with the boys from JLS. Both groups would normally stay for the spin-off show *The Xtra Factor*, which Caroline hosts, and JLS members Aston, Oritse, Marvin and JB were there on the sofa but the 1D boys were noticeably absent. Caroline introduced JLS as 'her favourite boyband' and no mention was made of Harry, Louis, Zayn, Niall and Liam.

The following night at London's five-star Corinthia Hotel, at the after-party to celebrate Little Mix's success – the first group to win the show – Caroline arrived with a male friend, presumably to try and divert scrutiny from her and Harry.

The cougar debate continued to roar, with one camp lauding her for bagging a hot young man, while the other named her a cradle-snatcher. It seemed that everyone and anyone were determined to have their say, and chat shows and newspaper articles quickly followed debating the cougar phenomenon. WAG Alex Curran waded into the furore, as did Kerry Katona, who chimed: 'If it's a Demi [Moore] and Ashton [Kutcher] situation, that's different because they're older. Harry is just a 17-year-old boy, so in my eyes it's just wrong. He's not long left school. He's not even allowed to drink yet.'

*

As Christmas drew nearer, the boys headed off on their much-anticipated Up All Night tour, opening with a warm-up gig at Watford's Colosseum. Caroline drove Harry to the venue in Hertfordshire and was seen waving him off with tears in her eyes.

The tour was a brilliant success. The boys bounded around the stage performing hits from their debut album – they say their favourite song is 'Up All Night' – and were met by a sea of screaming teens who hung on their every move.

The boys always have food and drink put in their dressing room backstage, but unlike other celebs don't demand the traditional rider featuring weird and wonderful things – like Madonna, who reportedly orders whole hotels to be repainted a different colour when she stays, while Mariah Carey apparently has someone in her dressing room just to pass her towels! The boys' requests are significantly less demanding and instead they just have drinks and sweets. Harry said: 'People put stuff in our room, but we don't go there and tell them what we need. Basically if you can get a cup of tea or bottle of water, it's fine.'

And their taste in riders has hardly moved on since then – Liam loves his Yorkshire Gold tea, while Niall prefers English Breakfast with three sugars in it and likes Irish sausages – though they were so impressed by the hot tub and sauna in their dressing room in Wolverhampton that they joked that they wanted the same facilities (and a communal dip) for each stop of their tour!

Harry has said that one of his rituals before performances is to change his pants. Playing such an extensive tour didn't go without its upsets, as poor old Harry continued to suffer from pre-show nerves that made him sick. 'He went through a period of throwing up before he went on stage,' revealed Liam. 'He's definitely the worst.'

The boys made sure each show was a personal experience for the assembled fans and each concert kicked off with a montage of words describing the dreamy summer holidays, such as 'skinny-dipping', 'kissing in the sunset' and 'parties on the beach'. As the video showed the boys headed to the beach in a camper van, there was a countdown of facts about each of them, with Harry being the first featured, revealing that he likes Milky Way crispy rolls and girls and dislikes white cars and beetroot.

The boys then came on stage and each took it in turn for a solo stint with their first track, 'Na Na Na', before launching into 'Stand Up', which they followed with 'I Wish'. Next they transformed the stage into a 1D beach party with the lads sitting around their orange and yellow campfire – harking back to the days in the bungalow – singing a medley of cover tracks including The Black Eyed Peas' 'I Gotta Feeling', Gym Class Heroes' 'Stereo Hearts', The Zutons' 'Valerie' and Natalie Imbruglia's 'Torn', while Niall jammed on his guitar.

This was followed by the ballad 'Moments', with a moonlit sea glowing in the background and finishing with images of fireworks exploding above them. Then came an old-fashioned video of the boys bounding into the super-posh Webberley College, where they clowned around in the library, common room and outside on bikes with girls from the school. Harry got to wear his famous bow tie, which he must have been delighted about. The whole look was really classy and had a vintage feel about it.

The set list continued with 'Gotta Be You', 'More Than This', 'Up All Night', 'Tell Me A Lie', 'Everything About You' and 'Use Somebody'. They would also do a shout-out of their favourite tweets and answer some questions from the networking site midway through the gig, often singling out girls who had travelled a long way to see them.

Another video followed of 'winter term', starting with a montage of words such as 'heading to Chamonix', 'snowball fights', and 'singing on ski lifts'. The boys were shown wrapped up in warm knitted jumpers as snow fell from the sky. The others dragged a sleepy Harry out of bed in their chalet and got ready for a day on the slopes. Cue lots of screaming at the topless shots!

'One Thing' and 'Save You Tonight' followed before they finished with their most popular hit, 'What Makes You Beautiful', when the audience's cries hit the roof. There was, of course, always room for an encore and as they left the stage after thanking the audience, another video was broadcast showing them dressing in their black suits for a celebration dinner, which the audience was invited to. They then burst into 'I Want'.

Costume changes ranged from casual prep to eveningwear tuxedos. Harry, who loves his blazer look, preferred to wear his navy jacket when performing but worked a casual white t-shirt equally well when teaming it with his trademark light-coloured chinos.

The boys' stylist Caroline Watson sourced the majority of their stage outfits from the high street including jeans for Harry from The Kooples, chinos for Zayn from River Island, striped t-shirts for Louis from Topman, Liam's checked shirts from Jack & Jones and Niall's preppy polo shirts from Ralph Lauren. Their footwear was mainly from Converse, Nike and Supra and they had some of the items custom made, including Harry's 'H' blazer and Zayn's varsity jacket.

Talking about his style on the tour, Harry told *Popdirt*: 'It's a lot of conversation about what we feel comfortable in, things we want to wear. Obviously people's style changes all of the time and she's very good at accommodating that. If you don't like something as much anymore and you might want to start doing something else, she's really up for changing it.' Harry cites his style icons as George Lamb, who he says dresses 'really sharp', and rapper Tinie Tempah.

They kept the choreography very simple, with no proper dancing, just basic blocking on the stage.

The tour was so tiring that all the boys had vitamin injections to boost their energy levels, with Harry deciding to have his in his bum! 'Four of us had to have vitamin jabs because we were run down,' he said. 'I do get homesick, too.' But they tried to ward off their exhaustion and homesickness by having fun and skated around the venues during their time off. They also played football and video games. Unsurprisingly, misbehaviour was always on the agenda. Harry said: 'We've all been having a lot of fun in the dressing rooms, getting up to mischief. Liam was asleep and Zayn shaved a slit in his eyebrow and I shaved my initials into his leg hair.'

The subject of Harry and Caroline was never far from people's minds and after they performed at the O2 Apollo in Manchester on 22 and 23 December they took time out of their busy schedule to talk to local radio station Real Radio. Presenter David Heane asked the five-piece: 'Well, I obviously have to ask about love lives and things that are going on so can we go around the group?' Each singer then said their name and declared their relationship status.

Niall said: 'I'm single, I'm Niall,' as did Zayn, while Louis and Liam both said they were off the market. Louis was dating model Eleanor Calder, who he got together with after splitting with Hannah the previous July, and by then Liam was with dancer Danielle Peazer. Harry, left until last, nervously said: 'I'm Harry, hello . . . Hi . . . Hi . . .' followed by a coy: 'I'm single.'

In an interview with the *Daily Record*, Harry contradicted himself and said that he and Caroline were 'really happy together' but then panicked and stuttered: 'I don't want to talk about my personal life.' However, when the journalist commented that they are media-trained, he shot back: 'Well, trained. Woo! You hear that?'

Of course traditionally boybands were banned by their

management from having girlfriends so they would appear 'available' to their fans and not alienate them. However, a decision was taken in the 1D camp that the boys could have relationships and be open about them – and there have been claims that they were encouraged to date older women as it was felt the fallout following any split would be less dramatic.

Spending so much time together, it's natural that the boys chat about their relationships and Harry says they spend 75 per cent of their time talking about women. 'We all give each other girl advice,' he told *BOP* magazine. 'If someone is having a problem with a girl, he'll come into the car and tell everyone about it. We all listen then give out advice and talk about it.'

Liam also revealed that Harry is the band's matchmaker, explaining: 'I actually got together with my girlfriend because Harry was the boy that set us up. Also, Louis and Eleanor as well, was also Harry. Harry's the magic match-up man.'

Harry was clearly very serious about Caroline and wanted to prove it to his family and friends, who are hugely impor-tant to him, so he took his girlfriend up to Cheshire to meet his family. Anne and Caroline were following each other on Twitter and Anne had even wished Caroline happy birthday on the social networking site back in November.

Christmas provided a much-needed break for Harry and the other boys and he headed home to Holmes Chapel for his 'ideal Christmas', one spent relaxing with his family, eating a really good Christmas meal and sitting in front of the TV. Harry joked that the lads were sending their guru Simon Cowell colouring books and crayons, while Louis added that they would be giving him some condoms. Caroline tweeted that she had bought Harry a car for Christmas, followed by the picture of a plastic toy one!

Harry wasn't going to have to rely on lifts from Caroline, his friends and mum for ever, because just before New Year, on 30 December, he was seen with a driving instructor outside his mum's house, waving to onlookers after passing the practical part of his test in a red Mini Cooper. Earlier in the month he had said it was his New Year's resolution to pass the test but he obviously managed to nail it before the start of 2012.

Liam was quick to congratulate him on Twitter. 'Massive well done harry!!!!!!' he wrote. 'Errmmmm Can I have a lift mate?' Niall wrote: 'Cmon @Harry_Styles get in! Smashes his drivin test.' And his sister Gemma joked: 'Awkward when your younger sibling passes their driving test before you ... Well done @Harry Styles! (a.k.a. My new chauffeur.)'

Harry's first motor was a black Range Rover Sport, with blacked-out windows, which he bought off his stepdad Robin. He then had to cough up £15,000 to insure it. He wasn't the only one of the group who came unstuck while insuring their car – Louis had treated himself to a Porsche the previous year but spent the same amount insuring it as it had cost him to buy it.

Gemma gave her first magazine interview in *Heat* that week, saying that she was supportive of Harry's relationship with Caroline and giving her the seal of approval. 'If he's happy, we're happy,' she said, adding: 'He's very thoughtful and caring. If he likes someone, he'll tell them. He won't hide what he's feeling.' However, she did say that he wasn't in love and has only had 'typical teenage relationships'.

His friends from home were also on his side, with Will saying: 'She's just Harry's girlfriend. It doesn't matter what age she is. As long as he's happy and doing his thing, that's all that matters.'

His father Des, however, was less pleased and said he thought the age gap was a bit 'extreme'.

Harry didn't see 2012 in with Caroline: she headed off on a sun-soaked month-long holiday to Goa in India with some friends. There were even reports that Harry had cried when she said she was going away for such a long time and that he had fallen for her really hard, while others claimed that the relationship had already fizzled out. It was thought that Caroline was planning to use the holiday to think about her priorities and whether she wanted to continue the high-profile romance. While they were both clearly very into each other, it seemed their every move was being scrutinised.

The boys had not long moved into flats in the same large building in London's Friern Barnet. Zayn, Niall and Liam had their own apartments but Harry and Louis – dubbed Larry Stylinson because they are so close – moved into one together, renting a luxury pad for £5000 a month. Ashley Cole had once lived in the same development, called The Dome, and it was where he met his now ex-wife Cheryl, who had also lived there.

Harry and Louis had a spacious living room with a long leather sofa and exposed brick walls, a second living room decorated in greys and whites, a 360-degree kitchen with a glass table in the middle for dining, and three bedrooms with king-size beds and en-suite bathrooms. Harry's room had a brown-and-cream colour scheme, with posters from clothes shops on the walls and clothes always lying around. The development also had a private health and fitness centre with a swimming pool, 24-hour security and a luxury cinema room showing all the latest films.

Louis said that he would only ever eat cereal or takeaway – and Harry would always ring him to tell him to come home for his tea. He said that they did normal stuff together. He told *Top of the Pops* magazine: 'Like a couple of weeks ago I made a cup of tea then went into bed with Harry and we watched a show called 50 Boybands of All Time.'

He had also landed himself a domestic partner in crime. 'I've loved cleaning since I was little, I find it very relaxing,' Harry told the *Daily Star*. 'I know it sounds weird and the rest of the lads tease me about it but I just really enjoy cleaning – what can I say? I'm happy to help out with anything, whether it's taking bins out, cleaning the kitchen or the bathroom.' Although his mum Anne begs to differ – and says he's very messy!

Louis hired a coach to bring fifty of his pals from his hometown of Doncaster down to their flat and, along with Harry's friends and the rest of the boys, they saw in the New Year together with a huge party.

Harry and Caroline were said to have wished each other a happy New Year via Skype and it was reported that Caroline had shed floods of tears as she spoke to her boyfriend who was thousands of miles away. Keen to keep his legions of fans happy, Harry still posted a series of pictures on Twitter of him, the boys and gaggles of female friends having fun together.

Caroline posted a message on Twitter, reading: '2011. What a year. The most important thing to me is love and happiness. Thankful for my incredible family and friends. Happy new year xxx.'

The 1D tour started back up again in Bournemouth on 3 January where the show was recorded for the DVD *Up All Night: The Live Tour*. When it was released it went on to top the charts in more than twenty-five countries.

However, the news emerged the same day that it wasn't just Caroline who was being subjected to abuse from 1D fans; some of the followers started to turn on each other when three girls who had been invited up on stage earlier in the tour in Watford became the victims of an online hate campaign. Hollie Gilbert was serenaded by Harry, who was wearing a tux at the time, during one of their songs. She immediately started getting nasty messages. One fan wrote 'you kinda rat-faced' and another said: 'You're not even pretty, why would Harry choose you?'

While the boys maintain that it is just a handful of Internet trolls that indulge in such behaviour, it is still a major issue and such is the fans' devotion that some girls would make it hell for others who got close to them.

And there were other mishaps; in Birmingham the boys were involved in an accident after a car sped into the band's tour bus. Police and ambulance crews were called and they said that three members of the group had headaches and back pain but their injuries weren't too serious. Twitter went crazy as fans tried to work out if they were all OK. Niall was quick to reassure them, writing: 'Guys, thanks for all your messages. We were involved in a really minor accident – we are all absolutely fine!'

The boys were advised to cancel their next gig at Plymouth Pavilions but didn't want to leave fans disappointed and went ahead anyway: a credit to the hard-working ethic that Simon Cowell recognised when he first signed them.

Around this time a naked picture which many claimed to be Harry was leaked on Twitter. It showed a curly-haired teen with no clothes on and silver dog tags similar to ones Harry wore, posing in the mirror, taking a photo of himself. The subject's face was obscured by the flash of the camera. Rumour spread like wildfire that it was Harry – especially because he liked to talk about being naked, but he denied it was him.

However, later in an interview with *We Love Pop* magazine, Harry joked that it would only take £100 for him to get his kit off. 'The thing is, if everyone has seen your willy, what have you left to surprise them with?' he said. Apparently he has even ridden a motorbike naked before!

Louis also confessed that the lads have all seen each other's private parts, and he's even caught Harry out. 'We've all seen each other's willies. Or do you mean, have we ever caught each other with a girl? I possibly, possibly, caught Harry once,' he said. 'I had an idea that something might be going on, so I thought it'd be banter to go in and ruin it. All I did was walk in and shout "Hello!" and then walk out. I'm such a kn*b.'

Caroline was spotted in London, back from her holiday, on 11 January, when the boys were playing Hammersmith Apollo. According to *Heat* magazine, the couple had a romantic reunion after the band's second night at the London venue. A 'source' said that the presenter drove to the venue just as the gig was finishing and according to onlookers some of the female audience started jeering and booing, while others were holding placards saying 'Flack off Caroline'.

The couple reportedly hung out with the rest of the group before heading back to Harry's flat to make up for lost time. There was also speculation that they were planning to go on holiday – perhaps a romantic ski trip – when the tour finished, to have some much-needed quality time together.

Caroline was seen accessorising with a black £130 Links of London friendship bracelet that Harry gave her before she went away on her trip to India. It was clear they were back together and just days later Caroline's twin sister Jody – who Caroline calls Jo – was seen dropping Harry off at King's Cross station as he headed up north for 1D's Sheffield gig. Her young children were in the back of the car. He gave Jody a friendly kiss before hopping out of her Audi, carrying an overnight bag.

However on 27 January, Harry confirmed he and Caroline had split – the pressure was just too much for them and the persistent attention had driven them apart. Harry was really upset but it seemed like they had no other choice. His hectic work schedule combined with the intense scrutiny meant they could no longer make it work.

After reports that he had dumped her, Harry insisted the decision was a joint one. On Twitter he wrote: 'Please know I didn't "dump" Caroline. This was a mutual decision. She is one of the sweetest, kindest people I know. Please respect that.'

And a few hours later, Caroline wrote on her Twitter: 'Lots of really sweet messages today … Thanks guys! Big hug with my new gloves :).'

Caroline held her head up high and presented ITV2's backstage coverage of the National Television Awards, with a new hairstyle. She tweeted 'my.head.hurts' the following morning, and a couple of days after that was photographed again with a group of friends enjoying a night out, trying to put the split and continual headlines behind her.

Harry was a few thousand miles away in Los Angeles and despite being surrounded by adoring fans at LAX airport, he kept his distance and looked downcast and miserable as he chatted on the phone.

Months later Caroline was still annoyed by the stories linking her with her ex, and hit out on Twitter: 'Note to some people/mags ... You are still speculating over something that clearly finished a while ago ... Leave it now ... Please.'

She eventually broke her silence when talking candidly to the *Mail on Sunday*. Caroline said that she and Harry remained on good terms and that they wanted to keep what had happened between them private. She revealed: 'Harry is adorable, he is a nice person. He was nice to me; we were nice to each other. We are still friends, he's brilliant, he is so much fun.'

She went on to explain how hard she found the press intrusion into her life, especially when photographers camped outside her mum's house and when she found herself constantly being tailed by paparazzi when she drove anywhere in the car. She did concede that she put herself in the public eye and has her dream job in front of the cameras, so it's to be expected to some extent.

She later told *Fabulous* that all the press attention around the time forced her to move house. 'At my old place, the front door opened straight on to the street,' she told the magazine. 'And when you walk out and you've got 20 men staring at you with cameras . . . it was embarrassing. I'd see my neighbours and say: "I'm so, so sorry."

'So eventually I decided to move east because I needed more privacy, which is what this place gives me. I feel much happier now. It never made me feel unsafe, it's just a real invasion of your life and everyone is entitled to a life.'

It was clear there were no hard feelings between them and Harry continued to tease her. During an interview with *OK!* magazine, he was asked to play a game of Snog, Marry, Avoid with Cher, Tulisa and Caroline. He said: 'Snog Cher, marry Tulisa and avoid Caroline! Caroline had really bad breath when we kissed. "Could do with a Tic Tac Flack", that's what I call her! Only joking.'

Even though the couple had both appeared to move on from their romance, it seems some of Harry's fans had not and Caroline still found herself subject to some vicious tweets. She was forced to go to the police when one fan sent a threatening picture of her wide eyed and carrying a knife.

Then she was the subject of a ridiculous hate campaign in an article aimed at young female fans in the magazine *One Direction & Friends*. Calling her 'grandma Caroline' the piece said that she had 'an outer hide that looks like leather', hair that looked like the 'ground of a petting zoo' and that she now spends all her time 'reading hate mail'. In a note to the 'voodoo doodoo' picture of Caroline, it added: 'Zero engagement rings because no one wants to be with her.' Poor Caroline was again forced to speak out about it and wrote on Twitter that it was one of the 'most hurtful things' she's ever read and that her 7-year-old niece, Willow, could write something more intelligent. She did say that she'd had some lovely messages from people when they read what had been written.

Much to everyone's surprise Caroline wasn't the only older woman in Harry's life. The previous August, before Caroline and Harry even got together, the boys were doing some promotional work around 'What Makes You Beautiful' and were interviewed on Manchester radio station, Key 103. Keen and confident, Harry caught the eye of married presenter Lucy Horobin, who was thirty-two at the time – fifteen years Harry's senior – and he started flirting.

Introducing the show, she said: 'I'm joined by five very handsome and lovely boys, and I've got you all to myself tonight.' Harry complimented her back, saying: 'You look lovely today,' and she replied: 'Thanks Harry, so do you.' A video shows that when she turned her back, Harry mouthed the words 'I love you' at her and was seen clutching his heart.

The romance didn't emerge until almost a year later but apparently the couple started exchanging flirty messages on Twitter and Facebook, finally meeting at a Manchester hotel where they consummated the relationship. Former colleagues revealed that they knew the pair hit it off immediately and that the secret affair was common knowledge among staff at the radio station.

Lucy had been married to her husband, Oliver Pope, for a year, and had also had a fling with Rizzle Kicks star Harley, who reportedly didn't know she was married at the time. Her husband later spoke bitterly to the *Sunday Mirror* about the breakdown of his marriage, putting full blame for the affair firmly at Harry's door. Oliver said that not long after the initial meeting between Harry and his wife, Lucy told him that she didn't want to be with him any more and that she no longer loved him.

He said: 'Days later Lucy went to a friend's party. She texted me to say she was staying on her mate's sofa and wouldn't be coming home, then changed her mind. A couple of hours later she got into bed with me. It gave me a glimmer of hope. But I've now discovered that's the first night she spent with Harry. She booked herself into a posh hotel in Manchester. He visited her around 2 a.m. Then she came back to our bed.'

Lucy – who is nicknamed Lulu by her friends – and Harry then went to see an Ed Sheeran concert and booked into another hotel.

Oliver – who had only bad things to say about the 1D star – added that he was humiliated because Harry was so much younger than him and he thought that it was unlikely his wife was the only woman Harry was seeing at that time.

In October, Lucy's relationship with Harry reportedly fizzled out after Lucy said she wanted to make a go of it with her husband. In February, they moved south after Lucy got a job on *Heart Solent* on the south coast. She later moved to London after bagging a role on *Heart Breakfast*.

When the news broke months later, it was only a matter of time before Harry's devoted fans took to Twitter, branding her a 'whore' and 'sick'. Lucy tweeted a sad face after one fan wrote: 'Haha you stupid f***ing wh**e. god you must have some issues to f*** a 17 year old boy haha-hahaha.'

She later tweeted: 'To clarify, I haven't said ANYTHING to any press, nor do I wish to. Thank you to those of you who have said kind words today. Xxx'. She was later forced to delete her Twitter account because of the volume of tweets.

Lucy then took a day off from work at Heart and her co-host James King explained the reasons behind her absence on their *Smooth Classics* show. 'Over the weekend you may have picked something up in the newsagents and read something which may have shocked you,' he said. 'I'd like to confirm the rumours are true and she has taken time off – to read *Fifty Shades of Grey* and tell us all about it tomorrow.'

A few months after the relationship with Harry went public, there were claims that Lucy and Oliver had decided to call time on their marriage but her spokesperson maintained that it was nothing to do with Harry. The statement read: 'Over the past few weeks both Lucy and her husband have agreed to end their marriage and decided to go their separate ways. The split has nothing to do with recent spec-ulation and they would request their privacy is maintained through this difficult time.'

Harry still maintains he likes an older woman – but would never date anyone older than his mum. He also admitted that he has read a bit of the erotic novel *Fifty Shades of Grey* after a friend forced him and he labelled the bestseller 'inter-esting' and 'educational'.

However, he told *The Sun* that he doesn't want to be seen as a womaniser and that he is often seen with girls who are just friends.

'It's fine, I have a lot of fun,' he said. 'I think that's impor-tant. You don't want to look back with any regrets, but at the same time if I met someone who I got on with and I liked then who knows? I know a lot of people are up for sitting down and going through who they have slept with. I know sometimes it might come across in the paper that I'm a bit like that, but I'm really not.'

Speaking to Radio 1 he also revealed that his 'dream cougars' were Angelina Jolie, Kate Moss and Kate Winslet. Kylie and Madonna were a definite no and if you want to capture his heart, he likes girls who wear black lingerie.

In another interview, he divulged what every 1D fan wants to know: his favourite position in bed. He says it's spooning and he likes to be the 'big spoon', although he doesn't mind too much. 'It also depends on the person you're with, because I had a girlfriend a while ago who pre-ferred to be the big spoon.'

However, any future girlfriend will have to put up with an intricate skincare routine. 'I wear so much spot cream at night,' he told the *Daily Star*. 'I have more than my mum.' You've been warned!

CHAPTER SEVEN

'We simply cannot believe that we are number one in America'

Cracking the American market is something all pop stars aspire too. Back in the 1960s, The Beatles invaded America and British rock and roll took the US by storm. In 1986, British artists like Duran Duran and Wham! accounted for almost a third of all records sold in the US. By 2002 just 5 per cent of music bought in the US came from artists signed in other countries – and UK stars are finding it harder and harder to make an impression across the massive nation.

Simon Cowell had started making plans for the boys to try and make it big in the States and had flown them to New York to meet record companies while they filmed the video for 'What Makes You Beautiful'. In November 2011, they signed a deal in North America with Columbia Records, home to Bob Dylan, David Bowie and Bruce Springsteen. Steve Barnett, the co-chairman, said that it wasn't a 'difficult decision' to sign the boys and while other boybands were slightly older, he thought there might be a gap in the market for them to succeed.

It was announced that they would support American boy-band Big Time Rush on their Better With U tour in their bid to crack the States. The tour would start in February 2012 and run through to the following month and 1D would release 'What Makes You Beautiful' on Valentine's Day and *Up All Night* in March.

Big Time Rush is a TV series on Nickelodeon about four hockey players who are selected to be in a boyband. It had the highest-rated live-action series debut and the group have sold thousands of records. A statement from One Direction read: 'We can't wait to hit the road with them in the US and having never been to New York before, the Radio City show is one we are all incredibly excited about!'

One Direction had picked a good time to compete in the US charts, with the likes of 'N Sync and the Backstreet Boys no longer around. Harry acknowledged the gap in the market, telling the BBC: 'I think for quite a while you know there weren't a lot of boybands even in the UK. I don't think there has been a massive boyband time recently.'

New Kids on the Block were less convinced that they would have success stateside. 'Even though the UK and England are big, it still sort of has a small town feel,' Joey

McIntyre told *Metro*. 'That's why you guys love your artists so much but boybands are so personality driven that sometimes it's about connecting with that and if the American girls don't connect with that swagger, it's hard.'

The power of social media meant they already had a head start and as soon as they touched down on American soil they had a visible and strong fan base. Thanks to the social media platforms of Twitter, YouTube, Facebook and Tumblr fans felt they were already connected with the boys, so the old-fashioned promotional slog across the country wasn't necessary. Together, the boys have notched up a massive 25 million followers on Twitter and Harry has the most with over 9.5 million. They also have their own YouTube channel.

Simon Cowell was so excited as the news spread in America and rather than his team putting pressure on the American labels, they decided to wait and see who got in touch with them. He wanted them to hear about the excitement from the media and fans, not in the traditional way.

He explained that the boys were very eager to have input into their marketing – and without them and their cheeky charisma, they wouldn't have the same levels of success.

The previous autumn an online marketing campaign had been launched by Syco and advertising agency Archibald Ingall Stretton (AIS). Targeting European fans, the multimedia adventure quickly spread to America. It involved twenty separate challenges featuring a central character called 1DCyberpunk who had stolen the band's laptop and would only give it back if fans proved they were as big a supporter as she was. Challenges included creating paper dolls of the boys, quizzes and singalongs.

Harry and the others spent three to five hours of their precious time creating videos of themselves, thanking fans for their work to help find the laptop and discussing their favourite entries. The final test was for fans to make videos of themselves running to the virtual listening party for the album.

The event culminated in the stolen laptop being found under a sofa and the album was broadcast to the 1D online community; fans across the world could hear the tracks while chatting to the band and each other. According to the Klout score, which measures how influential people are on social media, 1DCyberpunk was as influential as Victoria Beckham and had 2.5 million views on YouTube. Over fifty days, the traffic to the group's website doubled.

Richard Coggin, creative director at London agency AIS, said: 'Syco had a lot of great content – videos, merchandise, singles, albums, lyrics, running orders, signed photos, radio and TV appearances – and our brief was to glue it all together and engage the fans on a daily basis. Filtered through 1DCyberpunk, the content became more valuable and sought-after.'

As well as social media, the other huge Internet phenomenon is that of fan fiction, dubbed 'fanfic'. These are stories which amateur authors and fans self-publish on the web. Stories about the boys, especially Harry, dominate the sites and there are some sites dedicated to fan fiction just about him. As their fans multiplied, many flocked to these sites to create fantasies all about themselves and the band.

One girl, Emily Barker, even landed herself a publishing deal in 2011 after being discovered on Movellas. A publishing house signed her up after spotting that her story, entitled 'Loving the Band', about a boyband very similar to 1D, was the most popular on the site and that 30,000 Directioners had begged her to write more.

The boys are well aware of the stuff that is written about them, some of which is sexually explicit. After one fan wrote an intimate blog about going to see the boys, then pleasuring herself, Niall told *Digital Spy*: 'Yes I saw that! We see that sort of thing quite a lot. You can see girls are getting excited and they start crying or worse. In a lot of these countries they don't get a lot of gigs to go to, so when they see their favourite artist they take full advantage of it. Obviously the excitement builds up too much for some on the night and they get a bit . . . crazy.'

At the end of January and before the start of their tour alongside Big Time Rush they went back to LA and stayed their old haunt, the W hotel. Hundreds of fans camped outside and Harry was seen wandering topless by the pool in the sunshine. Without his shirt on fans could see another of his distinguishing features: his four nipples!

Harry once told *The Sun*: 'I've got four nipples. I think there must have been a twin, but then the other one went away and left his nipples behind.' However, this has never stopped him stripping off. 'I think you could safely say I'm not shy,' he said.

The new US Directioners found novel ways of trying to get to him. Harry said: 'We have had to use the hotel service lift. There are girls in the main lift the whole day, just going up and down hoping to bump into us.' However, Harry has always said that while some fans don't expect the boys to recognise them, they often do – and they enjoy getting to know the girls who follow them properly.

And the love across the pond for Harry was only just starting. He quickly caught the eye of one famous California girl – Arnold Schwarzenegger's daughter Katherine. She wrote on Twitter: 'Just watched my first One Direction video with my cousin and @HarryStyles is a cutie indeed!' Harry then apparently joked: 'Imagine having Arnie as your father-in-law,' before adding, 'Leave my house if you want to live' in his best Arnie accent.

The boys made a cameo stint on Nickelodeon sitcom *iCarly* alongside Miranda Cosgrove, and Katherine Schwarzenegger apparently jumped the queue to see Harry.

On Harry's eighteenth birthday on 1 February, reports emerged that he would be pushed to be the group's frontman as bands in America tend to do better with one very recognisable face to the fore. Funny, confident and with a good voice, apparently music bosses felt he was the most obvious choice. However, the boys refused and Harry made it clear he didn't want all the attention on him. The group decided to carry on as before with an equal share in vocals and input.

To mark his birthday in typical 1D style the boys

played a prank on Harry when they booked him in for a massage at the hotel spa. Letting the spa manager in on the joke, they waited until Harry was fully relaxed, with his eyes closed, then ran in and drenched him with buckets of iced water. They were all laughing and Harry vowed to get them back.

When asked if he felt different because he was eighteen, Harry laughed: 'I feel like I've woken up with suddenly more facial hair and a deeper voice.'

Arriving back in the UK on 9 February, he went straight to Manchester for a belated birthday celebration with his family. He went for a meal at the Italian restaurant Rosso, wearing a grey t-shirt, navy blue blazer and jeans.

The invitations were coming in thick and fast and Harry made his London Fashion Week debut the same week, appearing on the front row at Aquascutum's show at London's Savoy hotel. Harry had previously worn the brand for the cover of their *Up All Night* album. He was seen clutching an Aquascutum jacket and sitting alongside *X Factor* winner Alexandra Burke and young singer Dionne Bromfield. Also on the front row were James Corden and his fiancée, Julia Carey, and Harry and James seemed to hit it off brilliantly.

1D made a flying visit to Paris by Eurostar on Valentine's Day, signing copies of 'One Thing' at the Virgin Megastore there. While they were building their fan base in America, they still wanted to keep their European fans happy and they hadn't visited France on their previous trip across the continent. They were mobbed at Gare du Nord when they arrived. The boys had to hold on to bodyguards to make their way through the busy crowds and French police and soldiers were also on hand to keep the crowds at bay.

Harry wrote on Twitter: 'Hahaha Liam lost his shoe in the station. That was crazy!! Thanks for coming to see us.' And Zayn added: 'Had a sick day in France today. The fans were #crazy! Thanks to everyone who came to say hi :) x.' But love was obviously in the air and Harry wrote: 'Happy Valentine's Day!!! We couldn't do this if it wasn't for you . . . and we love you for that. Hope everyone has a lovely day! Oui Oui!!. Xx'.

On the way home Harry tweeted pictures of all his band-mates trying to get comfortable and sleep. On his return Harry went to The Groucho Club with Nick Grimshaw, who he was becoming increasingly chummy with, and Alexa Chung.

That same day 'What Makes You Beautiful' was released in America and charted at No. 28 – the highest *Billboard* Hot 100 debut for a UK act for fourteen years – and it quickly moved up the charts. The boys were proving so popular that they moved back the release date of *Up All Night*, after fans started to camp outside stores to get their 1D fix. Rather than releasing songs from it on the radio, the label mounted a 4-month-long marketing campaign to build a fan base via social media networks.

Johnny Wright, who managed New Kids on the Block, Backstreet Boys and 'N Sync, told *The New York Times*: 'Now they are calling the radio station, and the radio station is scratching its head, saying, "We don't even have that record yet." It's almost like the return of The Beatles. I call it hype, but it's positive hype because it's all real. It's not manufactured. No one paid these kids.'

Simon was particularly happy that rather than spending millions of pounds the news spread like wildfire for free via the Internet, showing the strength of the 'fan power'. However he did note that while social media worked for 1D, it only happened to the good groups, not everyone.

Next up was the music equivalent of the Oscars: the BRIT Awards. Held at The O2 arena and hosted by James Corden, the boys were nominated in the Best British Single category for 'What Makes You Beautiful'. James went over to the table where 1D were and the boys tried to hide the wine, beer and champagne that was on display. He then joked that they should be drinking squash, and asked Harry if he could confirm that he was dating Denise Welch. The very embarrassed singer said, 'It's true', before hitting his head on the table. The comedian then yelled: 'He loves a Loose Woman.'

The category was decided by public opinion and Capital FM listeners had been casting their votes for weeks. The boys were victorious, beating off Adele, Ed Sheeran, Jessie J, Example and the Military Wives, and picked up their Peter Blake-designed trophy.

Louis said: 'We cannot believe that we are stood here on this stage.' However, in a moment of confusion, Harry went on to thank the listeners of Radio 1. Six million viewers watching from home heard the mistake. Global Radio boss Ashley Tabor and his director of programming Richard Park were said to be displeased and an appearance on Capital was cancelled.

Radio 1 DJ Chris Moyles also tweeted: 'Best British single voted by listeners to Capital FM, One Direction. Harry Styles said "a massive thank you to Radio 1" HaHa Nice one!'

Mindful of the fact it might damage their chances of radio play on the channel their management quickly issued a statement, which read: 'One Direction forgot to thank the Capital Radio listeners last night when they were picking up their BRIT Award for "Best British Single". This was an oversight as the boys were so caught up in the excitement of winning. The band would like to take this opportunity to thank Capital Radio and all their listeners for their support and for voting for them.'

As the boys celebrated their win Harry tweeted: 'That was for all of you. Thank you so much. You're amazing. Now . . . Wooooooooooo!!!!!!!!!!!!' And although he was really embarrassed he put the slip behind him and went to the Sony after-party at The Arts Club on Dover Street, where he was pictured cosying up to Jo Wood and retail entrepreneur Harold Tillman.

Caroline Flack also attended the event but left soon after to head across town to the Universal party at the Soho House pop-up at Tate Modern with Nick Grimshaw and Rizzle Kicks.

The boys partied hard and when Harry left the venue he was rather the worse for wear. Perhaps made braver because of the alcohol he had consumed, he admitted on Twitter he did make the 'p*ssygate comment' to Matt Cardle at the *X Factor* final and apologised.

The following morning, in a chat with *Manchester Evening News*, he announced that he was going to leave his new gong in the loo. He laughed: 'You don't want to put it somewhere too show-offy, like in the hall or on your mantelpiece, so if you put it in the bathroom everyone's going to have to go in there at some point anyway!'

After a stern word from his management, he was also quick to apologise for the mistake he made on stage. 'Basically Radio 1 have supported us a lot from the start and in the heat of the moment I forgot to thank Capital, but we have thanked them now.'

He told the paper that in Holmes Chapel Harry-mania was so strong that there were always fans outside his house and his mum had to keep the curtains closed most of the time. He added: 'We get loads of love letters from fans pushed under the door because there isn't really a letterbox. But the weirdest find was a sanitary towel with my name written on it.'

Although her privacy was constantly being invaded Anne was delighted for Harry and he treated her as much as he could, buying her a silver Mini Cooper. She later came under fire for selling it on eBay and using Harry's name. She even promised to meet the eventual buyer of the car, as well as adding a picture of Harry driving the convertible, and she was inundated with messages from eager fans. Gemma admitted there were a few 'worrying' messages. 'You know its illegal to sell people?' she wrote on Twitter.

Anne missed Harry dreadfully and said that when he won The *X Factor* it was like 'empty nest syndrome'. However, she added: 'Now I can just walk into a newsagent and see a picture of him.'

Much as Harry missed his home life, it was clear that rather than slow down, his life was going to get even more hectic – some days the boys didn't know whether they were coming or going, or which country they would arrive in next. During their acceptance speech at the BRITs, Liam said that they were going to announce an arena tour and they unveiled a series of dates over a year away, kicking off at London's O2 arena on 22 February 2013.

Fans rushed to their phones and at one point a thousand tickets a minute were being shifted. They sold out within hours. There weren't enough seats, even though they were using venues with capacity for 28,000 fans, so they were forced to add extra dates in London, Cardiff, Manchester and Birmingham.

Their hard work was certainly paying off and the boys' earnings went through the roof. Reportedly they were set to make £64 million by the middle of 2013 on the back of ticket sales, world tours and their DVD.

'We fully expect to double that £32 million figure next year,' said the boss of Sony Music UK, Nick Gatfield. 'The team around them, including musicians, stylists, producers, tour managers and so on, is 90-strong,' he continued. 'That's 90 jobs created by these five boys.'

However, according to biographer Tom Bower, in his book *Sweet Revenge: The Intimate Life of Simon Cowell*, the boys had actually netted even more. He wrote: 'One Direction were Cowell's new Westlife – a revival of his mastery of the music business. Nothing had been left to chance by Sony Music with the band's album *Up All Night* selling over 5 million copies. The songs, publishing, discs, DVDs, merchandising and endorsements brought in huge profits with the five members of the group estimated to have earned nearly £100 million. Naturally Sony and Syco raked in much more.'

Zayn is said to have paid out £2.2 million for a new house, whereas Louis spent a bit more on a five-bedroom pad in north London for £2.5 million. However, curly-haired Harry was being a bit more careful with his earnings and had shelled out just £575,000 for a large, one-bedroom east London property, which featured a Japanese zen garden with panoramic views over London and apparently had a cool blue front door.

'Harry's new pad is amazing but the garden is the best bit,' a 'source' told *The Sun*. 'He says it'll be perfect for summer parties and barbecues.'

Their first date supporting Big Time Rush was on 24 February in Chicago at the Rosemont theatre. The boys pulled out a polished show and fans – dubbed US Directioners by Niall – set the tone as they screamed the house down. The boys had been styled in an all-American look with red, white and blue being the theme – Harry wore a white t-shirt, white trousers and navy blazer.

Apparently they were such a hit with the audience that a large number walked out after their set and weren't interested in seeing the main attraction, Big Time Rush.

Two days later, on 26 February, they performed at the Air Canada Centre in Toronto and toronto.com wrote: 'Interestingly, when One Direction left the stage after seven songs, a noticeable portion of the crowd joined them ... Despite BTR's Herculean 75-minute effort, it seemed most fans preferred the simpler approach of the warm-up act – or should we say, co-headliner – One Direction ... At least one band's career direction is on the rise. Bieber beware, and parents, guard your wallets.'

While they were in Canada they did a whistlestop promotional tour and officials were forced to shut down the street outside the Toronto headquarters of MuchMusic when the band stopped by to make their first appearance on Canadian television. Harry later revealed that one poor girl was crushed against the barrier and looked like she might have broken her leg; their tour manager Paul went to rescue her. Harry and Louis said that they tried Canadian favourite poutine – chips with gravy and cheese – which they said they enjoyed.

Harry dismissed rumours about playing Mick Jagger in a

film, saying he's 'not a very good actor'! 'Did you not see *iCarly?*' he asked the presenter.

As well as causing chaos during their MuchMusic appearance, the boys conducted interviews with press inside The Ballroom Bowl, where they joked around with assembled fans who had tracked them down at the venue.

News of their success in North America quickly reached home, with Lily Allen tweeting her congratulations to the boys. She wrote: 'Its amazing how well One Direction are being received across the pond, no? Good luck to em I say, seem like good lads.'

And Paul McCartney said: 'Let's just call them the next terrific band. Doing well in America – good luck lads.'

The quintet were overwhelmed by the support of fans across the pond and Harry told *The Sun*: 'To come over here and see that so many people know all the songs on an album that isn't even out yet is unbelievable. Not many people get to do what we do in England, so for us to come over here and be able to perform to crowds like this is amazing and humbling.'

He added that one fan had been following them around America and was trying to lure them for a night out!

Bill Werde, a representative from *Billboard* magazine, said: 'There's a lot of possibility here, there's a lot of upside ... that level of talent with those kinds of looks ... it's really a perfect storm for a massive, massive successful phenomenon.'

They continued touring around the States as the supporting act to Big Time Rush and travelled mostly on the 1D bus, which has rarely been pictured in the media. According to 1D, the plush van had a 'sleepover' vibe and they would pass the long journeys playing the football video game FIFA – with Harry battling it out with Louis to be the best. They also tuned in to their favourite TV shows like *Family Guy, American Dad, The Jeremy Kyle Show* and *Sun, Sex and Suspicious Parents*.

Liam labelled the bus 'disgusting' and likened it to a student residence – and said Harry was the second messiest after Louis. While they were on the road, pizza and Asian food became firm favourites.

Harry told *Teen Now* that there aren't many rules on the bus, only 'clean up after yourself, naked at all times, get up at 9.30 every day – maybe 10 and only one glass of milk before bed.' However, he does say the things that annoy him while they are on the road are Louis' smelly feet; that Niall 'trumps' a lot; and the fact that Liam has no patience and 'cannot wait to do stuff'. The most irritating thing about Zayn, Harry told *The Edge*, is the fact he just sits there and pouts!

The boys have their little rows, but it never gets serious and Harry says the worst that has ever happened was when he hit Louis with a shoe. He told Virgin Radio 96: 'I think because we spend so much time together any fights are brotherly squabbles. It's about what radio station we listen to, or what we're having for lunch. They're over in five minutes.'

On 1 March, the group travelled on as a four-piece after Harry announced that Zayn had had to pull out following the death of his aunt. He headed back home for her funeral in the UK and the 1D fan base rallied around. They hated to think about his grief, especially after the death of his grandfather during the *X Factor* show. In true Directioner style, #StayStrongZayn quickly became a trending topic on Twitter. Zayn didn't comment but retweeted a message, which read: 'God has no Phone, but I talk to him. He has no Facebook, but he is still my friend. He does not have twitter, but I still follow him.'

After a few performances without him, they were happy to have him back when he joined them in New York a little over a week later. They tried to boost his spirits. Harry tweeted a picture of a grinning Zayn sticking his tongue out and posing in sunglasses, accompanied with the caption: 'Like he never left.' Then he said: 'Off to a radio interview . . . first show tonight with Zayn back . . . It's gonna be fun :)'

Zayn has always commented on Harry's caring nature and the fact he asks if he's OK when he's down and even calls him 'my rock'. Louis also admitted that Harry would be the person he went to.

He added: 'Any day I need a cuddle I'll knock on Harry's door and give him a big hug. The majority of the time I do go to Harry if I'm a bit down because I'm really close to him and we understand each other. Liam's also a great guy to comfort you.'

The boys were becoming quite the in-demand stars in the States and while they were in New York on 8 March they were guests of honour at the premiere of the new Nickelodeon film *Big Time Movie*, starring Big Time Rush. It was Zayn's first public appearance since his sad family news and he looked relaxed and happy surrounded by his bandmates on the orange carpet. They said they were having a lot of fun on the tour with the Nickelodeon stars.

The following day, after their final gig supporting Big Time Rush at Radio City Music Hall, the boys had a mad experience when they were caught in traffic, even though the police had blocked the road for them, and girls surrounded the car. Then the boys got into trouble when they got a bit rowdy during a game of bowling and broke the machinery on their lane.

Louis said: 'The whole thing came off its hinges. It totally broke. We got a slap on the hand and were told off by the label for that. We'd taken over a lane, played about two games and then got a bit bored. So we started an experiment, throwing two or three balls at the same time.' Harry joked: 'It was really bad but quite funny – but no one else thought so.'

And boys will be boys: during a visit to Elvis Duran's Z100 *Morning Show*, the boys were presented with a cake to congratulate them on their massive success and Zayn and Louis slam dunked Harry's face in it, leaving him smeared with blue and red icing.

He later tweeted: 'I just got caked in the face . . . and a cake made of ice cream is harder than regular cake. Hard cake in the face.'

Harry says that they get into trouble about five times a day normally – being well behaved is not one of their traits!

Three days later they landed a slot on America's biggest breakfast programme – *Today*, on the NBC channel – where the presenter said they were 'inspiring the next case of Beatlemania'. 'Odds are if you have a teenager in your house, a pre-teen girl, she's already obsessed with One Direction,' she said.

As the boys arrived in an open-top red bus for the show at the Rockefeller Plaza, they were mobbed by an estimated 10,000 fans, most of whom were carrying banners. Many of the crowd, thought to be the largest for any of the show's outdoor concerts, had camped out for a number of days and the boys had been out to see them and handed them some refreshments.

For their first performance on American TV, which was watched by around 5 million people, they sang 'What Makes You Beautiful', 'One Thing' and 'More Than This'.

During the interview Zayn told the show's hosts, Ann Curry and Matt Lauer: 'Since we got put together, we've made four best friends, you know, we've lived together, we're on the road and we do something that we love every single day, so for us that's the most amazing part. The only downside is we don't see our friends and family as much as we'd like to but other than that, you know, we're just enjoying everything that, you know, life is throwing at us at the minute.'

They also announced that they were following in the footsteps of Justin Bieber, the Spice Girls and Katy Perry and would be starring in their own 3D film, to be released at the end of 2013. The scripted comedy will reportedly net them £50 million. Justin Bieber's *Never Say Never* grossed a whopping £60 million at the box office.

It was later announced that it would be directed by the man who made his name with the Oscar-nominated documentary *Super Size Me*, Morgan Spurlock, who would portray the boys 'in a whole new light' and blend behind-the-scenes footage with concert material.

Simon Cowell told MTV News: 'Well, I mean, for anyone who's a fan of the band you're gonna get the chance to see what it's like preparing for these big concert tours, a lot of it is about the fans.'

Commenting on the decision to have Morgan at the helm, he added: 'He's cool, I met him. I think it's gonna be amazing . . . He's just such a fan of doing it.'

Morgan explained: 'This is an incredible opportunity and an amazing moment in time for the band. To capture this journey and share it with audiences around the world will be an epic undertaking that I am proud to be a part of.'

Harry said it would be a good chance for his fans to get up close and personal, explaining: 'The film could be exciting. My hair could be poking in your eye.' He also said that cameras have been following them for a while and he was looking forward to watching back the incredible time they've been having when he is older.

The New York Times claimed that while they were in the States, Harry started seeing 19-year-old US performer Lily Halpern, who is best known for her viral video of Nicki Minaj's song 'Starships'. The pair were introduced through Big Time Rush, who Lily had supported on tour the previous year. They met after she went to see the boyband perform.

The pretty brunette star was seen leaving Harry's hotel room but in an attempt to avoid publicity around it, a 1D spokesperson denied the claim they were dating, saying: 'Never heard of her. Harry is single.'

However, Lily later spoke to *Heat* magazine and said they had hung out together while Harry was in New York and watched films, including family favourite *Flubber*!

'He's a really really great guy,' she said, adding, 'Harry's funny and he's an honest guy. He doesn't take things too seriously so we can tease each other.' Lily – who said she knew they weren't in an exclusive relationship at the time – refused to answer when she was asked if she had kissed him, yelping: 'Help me. No comment.' She also said that they stayed in touch throughout the rest of the tour and texted each other regularly when the boys left.

She told *E! News*: 'Like, who doesn't have a crush on Harry Styles? I don't know, yeah. He's great. He's a good friend, he's a very good friend.' She then hinted that their managers were talking about her collaborating with them. She said it would be too hard to have a relationship because they were both so busy. She also received hatemail – but said she has a thick skin. 'It's not anything that I can't handle,' she continued. 'I think they're just protective of him and of the whole band. Their fans are so passionate about the band – they want to make sure anyone he's involved with is good enough for him. I promise I'm a good friend to him!'

But it seems that Harry was most definitely still acting like a single guy and when the group turned up at the Q102 radio station in Philadelphia for more promotional activities, he made a shameless attempt to get the attention of curvy Kim Kardashian by carrying a poster of the reality star in a bikini. On it, he had stuck a post-it note with the words, 'Call me, maybe?' He also added a smiley face for good measure.

And it wasn't just Harry who was keen to get to know the famous Kardashians. Niall had already tweeted Kim's sister Khloe when the band played in Texas, asking her to their gig there, but he also made sure he invited her husband, American basketball star Lamar Odom. However, Khloe replied that sadly they weren't around that night.

He may not have immediately got his wish of a date with Kim, but the boys were given adorable puppies to cuddle ahead of performing an acoustic set on the station.

The album *Up All Night* was released in North America on 13 March and, unbelievably, made transatlantic history on 20 March when 1D became the first UK pop group to debut with a No. 1 in the US *Billboard* album chart. The previous highest entry for a UK group was the Spice Girls with their album *Spice*, which only got to No. 6 in 1997. The boys were delighted and shocked. This kind of success was beyond their wildest fantasies.

Harry said: 'We simply cannot believe that we are number one in America. It's beyond a dream come true for us. We want to thank each and every one of our fans in the US who bought our album and we would like to thank the American public for being so supportive of us.'

Understandably, Simon and the rest of the Syco team were also over the moon. Simon tweeted: 'I couldn't be happier for One Direction, it is an incredible achievement. They deserve it. They have the best fans in the world.'

Cheryl Cole was quick to quip that she had mentored the boys when Simon wasn't there, jokingly taking credit for their success.

Caroline Flack wrote: 'Incredible news for One D!!!! HUGE news x', and Olly Murs wrote: 'WELL DONEEEEE!! @onedirection #1 with Debut Album in US Billboard Charts!! 1st Ever Uk Band to do it!! That's amazing stuff lads!! Ledge!!'

JLS wrote: 'Congrats to One Direction on their US no1 album. That's HUGE boys well done! Marv and the lads.' And Katy Perry took time to single out Niall, who she had put through in the early stages of *X Factor*, to say well done to him.

Harry celebrated by buying himself a new mattress – so rock and roll! 'I needed a new one, the springs had gone,' he explained, not doing much to stop his reputation as a womaniser.

The news went global and journalists everywhere were quick to comment on the recipe for their success.

Music Week journalist Paul Williams said: 'It's more than unusual, it's unprecedented,' and explained that being managed by Simon helped boost the band's profile.

'He [Cowell] has a hell of a lot to do with it. He is one of the most famous people on TV in America and he's been associated with Leona Lewis and Susan Boyle, both of whom have had number one albums in America, so he has a lot of influence. When Simon Cowell drives an act, people are going to listen and pay attention. Although you have got to have the goods, as well as having someone like Simon championing you.'

Ernie D, the creative director of Radio Disney, said that bands like The Wanted and 1D were becoming popular much more quickly than their predecessors in the 1990s because of social media.

'The way it's happening now, it's a little more sudden. Back then, you had to build your fan base, get a following. Now with all social media, you have a fan base immediately. Bands like One Direction and The Wanted, they're just coming out of nowhere and it's kind of taking everybody by surprise.'

The group were inducted into the *Guinness Book of Records* for this incredible accomplishment. The album would go on to top the charts in sixteen countries, including Australia, Canada, Ireland, Italy, Mexico and New Zealand. It was a huge moment not just for them but for UK music as a whole and for the return of boybands, who were dubbed as 'hot' once again. UK band The Wanted were also proving popular stateside and their single 'Glad You Came' peaked at No. 4 on the *Billboard* Hot 100.

Rivalry was starting to simmer between the two bands. Max George, Nathan Sykes, Tom Parker, Jay McGuiness and Siva Kaneswaran first hit the States a few months before 1D in an attempt to boost their career. As well as landing a top ten spot with their single, they revealed that they were in talks to star in their own reality TV show, similar to the one that girlband The Saturdays were making.

The feud initially started between them and 1D when they were asked if the bands were friends. Frontman Max replied: 'We're not the best of friends, so it's not like we're going to go up and start hugging and kissing. And they make little comments in interviews when we're mentioned. But they're young, and that's expected, and I laugh at it. If they're taking it seriously, then maybe that's just an age thing.'

He then threw down the gauntlet when he heard they would be crossing the pond to try and crack the States, initially by telling *The Sun*: 'Our song is No. 4 in the charts. Maybe when they have a song right next to us in the charts over there, they'll be competition. Whenever you say anything about One Direction their fans get a little bit angry. I guess because they're quite young.'

However, it didn't go down well in the 1D camp and Louis hit back in an interview with *Now* magazine.

'I just think, "If you want to create that rivalry, then let's do it." We're not bothered about the friction or the rivalry. But I'm not going to shy away from it because that isn't the person I am. I don't think it's fair to me or any of the lads.'

A few months later Louis was spotted reading their book in a pound shop, making sure he was pictured whilst flicking through the pages.

Then Max reignited the feud during an interview on Radio 1 after some gentle ribbing from DJ Chris Moyles, when he said The Wanted's new music wasn't 'stereotypical' and Harry hit back with a spot of banter on Twitter, writing: 'Chris Moyles is actually right though . . . If 1D aren't in the picture, The Wanted would've been WAY more popular!'

The fight continued to rumble on when Zayn commented on a picture of Max, calling him a 'geek'. When Max replied, saying, 'Does that mean I'm "in"?' Zayn tweeted: 'I'm not sure why your still talking to me mate conversation ended when I called you a geek. p.s your display just [s]how's how much of a wannabe you are :)'.

Max sarcastically replied: 'That's not very nice. I was just starting to like you and your RnB hits.'

Tom Parker then waded in and said to Max: 'I think "1 stripes" got his knickers in a twist bro,' and Zayn attacked him saying: 'if I had a face like yours my hair would be the last thing I'd worry about :).'

Max had the last word and said: 'Enjoy rehearsals. Stay off the bud . . . It clearly makes u cranky.'

But Zayn wouldn't let it rest and later referred to Max

as 'chlamydia' boy just days after he split from his fiancée, *Coronation Street* actress Michelle Keegan, after reportedly cheating on her. Michelle had been spending time with Zayn's girlfriend, Little Mix's Perrie Edwards.

Max hit back, writing: 'Tell me you're problems without the 8 security in NYC. The only problem I have with you is the s*** banter. Grow up son.'

During the American tour, Max told Channel 955: 'I'm not sure what his problem is to be honest. It started off that I thought we were just having a bit of banter, but he seemed to get a bit serious. I tried to palm it off as being friendly again, but you can only take so many insults and eventually I just said, "Alright listen – if you've got a problem, come and see me in New York when we're there doing a gig together and we'll sort it out."'

His bandmate Jay also commented on Zayn's allegations of Max having an STD: 'It's like when kids in the playground go "Poo Breath!" – rarely has that kid actually eaten faeces. I think he was just taking a stab in the dark.'

1D's first performance after landing the No. 1 spot was in Dallas and a security team of one hundred was employed to keep the boys safe. Even though they only played four songs at the open-air Dr Pepper Ballpark as part of their promotional blitz, it seems that their team was taking no chances.

From there, they headed to Montreal, where a number of fans were hospitalised after trying to catch a glimpse of the boys before their gig at the MusiquePlus studio. The hardcore fans camped out in freezing temperatures, which dipped to a low of minus 10 degrees Celsius, and ambulance workers reportedly had to treat fourteen of them. Six fans were allegedly taken to hospital to be treated for conditions ranging from fainting to mild hypothermia.

In the interview, Harry said that he was loving travelling the world with four of his best friends – and that even when they're not working they hang out with each other – and that he loved Liam's bushy eyebrows!

At the end of March, the group attended the star-studded Nickelodeon Kids' Choice Awards in Los Angeles, where they sang 'What Makes You Beautiful'. Luckily for them, they even made it off the stage slime-free! The boys wore monochrome black and white – Harry in his blazer, Louis with his braces, Liam wore a checked shirt, Zayn sported a Varsity jacket and Niall was dressed in a black collared t-shirt.

There was a very important guest in the crowd, Michelle Obama, who was seen dancing away to the track alongside her two daughters, Malia and Sasha. Harry said he had 'too much respect for Barack' to comment on his wife's appearance when he was asked, while Liam was happy to rate her as eleven out of ten.

After the show the First Lady invited them to the White House for the annual Easter egg hunt – and Harry made her laugh by asking how they ordered pizza from the White House. Sadly, due to their commitments the boys weren't able to take up the exclusive invite, but if they ever needed confirmation that they had made it, this was it.

Harry later admitted it was the 'maddest celebrity moment' and wrote in the band's official 2013 annual: 'She was so nice and cool, and her kids were comfortable with talking to people they don't know.'

The boys were in a prime spot at the awards show and sat in the front row alongside the likes of Halle Berry and Heidi Klum. Katy Perry, Selena Gomez, Justin Bieber and Taylor Swift also turned out for the event.

Everyone had an opinion about them, and fellow Brit Kelly Osbourne said: 'They are so amazing and they are so lovely and it makes me so happy – it's like the Brits taking over. I love it.'

US *X Factor* finalist Rachel Crow commented: 'I love them, they are amazing and their songs are amazing and they are the nicest of guys. I love them all, my favourite changes daily.'

Justin Bieber said: 'The single guys from One Direction are going to have a lot of fun. They sound great and when you add their British accents into the mix, the American girls are going crazy for them. Sure, you need the talent, but you need to win over the American public – that is what it is all about. One Direction are genuine good guys. The industry needs a fresh boyband and by the end of this year, they will be the biggest boyband in the world.'

The boys were blown away by the reception and Harry tweeted: 'I feel incredibly lucky to have the life I do . . . I met some amazing people today. And had a lot of fun. Thank you so much. x'.

It was another highlight to add to their increasing list of wonderful experiences.

Afterwards the boys managed to take time out of their hectic schedule – it had been non-stop for weeks – and they were seen relaxing in the sun at the W hotel, where they were staying. Liam's dancer girlfriend Danielle tweeted a picture of herself, showing her man topless and Harry, who was wearing sunglasses and looked like he was reading. It can't be easy being the girlfriend of one of the guys and Danielle, who met Liam when 1D were on *The X Factor*, has been subject to some abusive tweets.

She had been spending time with Louis' girlfriend, model Eleanor Calder, and the previous week she had tweeted: 'the people at the pool taking photos [of] me and Eleanor . . . we can see you. Please don't, we're not even that interesting :) Thank You xxx.'

As Louis' relationship with Eleanor got more serious he lashed out at rumours that he and Harry were in a gay relationship, saying it was 'degrading' to Eleanor. He said in an interview on Tumblr: 'This is a subject that was funny at first but now is actually hard to deal with as I am in a relationship. Me and Harry are best friends, people look into our every move. It's actually affecting the way me and Harry are in public. We want to joke around but there seems to be a different rumour every time we do anything.'

He added: 'I act the same way with Harry as I do any of the other boys and my childhood friend Stan.'

He also moaned to *Now* magazine: 'A lot of them are so

wrapped up in the conspiracy. Let me tell you now, they'll find a way to put a twist on this interview. Yeah [it upsets me]. I think it's pretty obvious when you see me and Eleanor together that it's real.'

The boys also said that the images of them kissing are photoshopped.

Harry, meanwhile, wasn't letting his reputation as a womaniser go to waste and was apparently snubbed by 32-year-old *Bachelorette* star Jillian Harris after he asked for her number while they were at a restaurant.

'He asked for my phone number,' Jillian told the *Sunday Mirror*. 'He looked cute and adorable. But he was also very young looking. I am sorry but I could never date an 18-year-old. I don't think that's even legal in the US is it?'

She did concede that if she was twenty-one, the situation would've been very different but that Harry didn't seem too put out.

During this time, Simon Cowell started setting the wheels in motion, challenging the world's most successful song-writers to write music for the band's next album. After the runaway success of *Up All Night*, they didn't want to suffer from the notorious 'second album syndrome'. Syco bosses enlisted the help of writers for Britney Spears, Kylie, Madonna and Katy Perry, who started working on potential chart-toppers. Importantly, the boys would also get their say on what they wanted.

Their next stop in the US was back in New York, where they were pictured looking exhausted as they touched down at JFK airport. They appeared on another huge US TV programme, *Saturday Night Live*, with *Modern Family* star Sofia Vergara. They sang 'What Makes You Beautiful' and 'One Thing'. Starring on this show is seen as a rite of passage for celebrities and it is enormously popular with viewers.

Harry had been asked before the show whether he would get with Sofia if he could and he replied yes, without hesitation! The actress was clearly enjoying her time with the boyband and took to her Twitter account to gush about how much fun she was having with them, saying they were 'sooo funny!' Harry meanwhile, was also excited by the fact that Hollywood actress Kate Beckinsale was in the studio.

Their sketch showed the boys sporting moustaches and wigs and dressed in flamboyant shirts, putting on their best Spanish accents as they pretended to be Sofia's children on the fictional *Manuel Ortiz Show*.

While in New York, Harry was linked to another older brunette. The lady in question this time was 24-year-old Irish photographer Sarah-Louise Colivet. The pair apparently hooked up on a couple of occasions and vowed to keep in touch. Her mother Jacinta said: 'It's true, she has struck up a friendship with him. She rang and said he was lovely, great fun and a really nice guy.'

'What Makes You Beautiful' was covered by the cast of popular show *Glee*, further proving One Direction's success in the States. The song featured in the Prom-a-saurus episode.

A thrilled Niall said: 'To have a song in *Glee* is just fantastic. We're all big fans of the show and are so excited they chose "What Makes You Beautiful" for an episode.'

The only negative moment from their time in America was when an American group of the same name came forward and tried to sue them for $1 million. The US group filed a lawsuit against the UK band, asking them to change their name. In the documents it said that they had formed in 2009, a year before Harry and the boys.

Harry insisted their name would stay the same and, asked what would happen, Zayn replied: 'We don't have any idea but we're not changing our name.'

A 1D spokesperson said: 'There is a dispute with a local group in California about the ownership of the One Direction name in the US. One Direction's management tried to resolve the situation amicably when the matter first came to light, but the Californian group has now filed a lawsuit claiming they own the name. One Direction's lawyers now have no choice but to defend the lawsuit and the band's right to use their name.'

They argued that the lesser-known group – who were led by singer and pianist Sean O'Leary and played at local fairs and bars – were trying to ride on the coat-tails of their success.

The warring parties eventually settled. 1D were allowed to keep their name and the American group would use the moniker Uncharted Shores. Directioners could breathe easy once again.

CHAPTER EIGHT

'Everyone was saying we weren't very rock 'n' roll . . . I thought I'd throw a TV out of the Winnebago window'

With fans popping up all over the world, the group's next stop was Australia for their Up All Night tour, which they had started in the UK at the end of 2011 and had taken a break from to promote their music in the US. In preparation for their visit, a special store opened in Sydney selling nothing but 1D merchandise: dolls, CDs, t-shirts, hoodies and posters. Girls camped out overnight to be the first to get their hands on the products.

They arrived after a long flight on Easter Monday and were ushered from the plane by security guards. Sadly for the hordes of waiting fans, they slipped quietly through the back door into waiting blacked-out cars. These were tailed by eager followers, trying to catch a peek of the famous boys. They checked into the five-star Sydney InterContinental and a few lucky onlookers were rewarded for their patience when a topless Zayn walked past the window. Harry fans weren't so happy as he kept his white t-shirt on.

On their first full day, they had some rare time off and spent a few hours relaxing on a luxury yacht in the famous harbour, enjoying some cold beers after weeks of abstinence in the US, where the legal drinking age is twenty-one. Harry stripped down to his low-slung, brightly coloured swim shorts and showed off his gorgeous abs as he took a boat ride with Zayn and Louis, while Liam tried his hand at fishing.

Harry displayed his impressive diving skills when he launched himself into the water to cool off. It was some much-needed downtime and Niall tweeted: 'Sick time today, having a right laugh, out swimming. Chilling bigtime today, @real_liam_payne went fishing and caught the boat.'

There wasn't just performing in their busy diaries – as well as the shows, they were doing as many interviews as ever. The following morning they made a guest appearance on *Sunrise* on Channel 7 and it was more of the same as hundreds of fans gathered on Martin Place so they could have front-row positions outside the studio. Some were so hysterical that local police were forced to erect metal fencing to stop them surging forward, and several fans were so overcome by excitement that they just keeled over and were hoisted out of the crowds and given immediate medical treatment. The hosts even asked the boys to gesture in unison for them to move back, to try and get through to them.

When asked how they were coping, Harry replied that they were taking it in their stride. He said: 'I think for us, it's not something we have to cope with. We're teenage boys having an amazing time.'

It would appear that tasting the local dishes would always be part of their world travels and while they were on the show, Harry tucked into an Australian delicacy, a meat pie with relish.

But as bedlam continued to reign outside, the boys were concerned about their fans' safety and Niall tweeted: 'Guys this is crazy here, thank you all so much! Please stay safe, the police here have been amazing, we don't want anyone to get hurt.'

The boys chatted to a number of radio stations and, in an effort to change the questions and vary the format, when they went on *The Kyle and Jackie O Show* on 2Day FM, they answered questions after sucking on helium balloons! Harry sounded particularly high-pitched after gulping some of the gas and Louis and Zayn admitted they had snuck out to explore the city.

Zayn shared: 'We got lost in Sydney, just roaming the street looking for friends.'

'Yeah, true, it was just like a smash and grab ... It's not

like we snuck out at 2 a.m., it was like 8 p.m., which is past our bedtime anywhere . . .' Louis added.

However, for all the faithful fans, there were always some girls who would turn on one another if it seemed that the boys were getting close to them. When they appeared on radio station Nova FM, they met 20-year-old receptionist Anna Crotti. On air Harry said she was 'lovely' and 'very polite', and Zayn said she had 'beautiful eyes'.

Zayn later asked her out after getting one of their entourage to ask for her number. However, she was forced to cancel their date after she was bombarded with abuse on Facebook.

Anna told the *Mirror*: 'By the end of the day, it got a bit too scary. Random girls were abusing me on Facebook. Girls were calling the radio station and giving me s**t. Mothers even called me in tears, demanding to know if I knew where One Direction were because their daughters wanted to meet them. I didn't even want to walk home. It was so intense.'

Harry also hit on reporter Ellie Halliwell, who confessed that he'd approached her after she interviewed him.

She wrote: 'I did notice during my Wednesday interview with the band that Styles was staring at me, but I was surprised and flattered when a member of the publicity team rang me to ask if Harry could have my number.' However, she turned him down because she was engaged!

They were working very hard but Harry was determined to have a good time and he and Zayn surprised bar-goers when they turned up at The Scary Canary, a backpacker bar close to Darling Harbour in Sydney. They were in the cordoned-off VIP section but were happy to dance and mess around with fans.

Early the following morning Louis and Liam tried their hand at surfing on Manly Beach but Harry and Zayn were only too pleased to stay in bed, presumably to sleep off the heavy night before. They felt happy that they could have a relatively normal lads' night out, even though everyone knew who they were.

The next day the boys, supported by local singing sensation Johnny Ruffo and *Australia's Got Talent* winners Justice Crew, performed their first-ever Australian gig at the Hordern Pavilion. Apparently only 60 per cent of the people waiting to get into the venue had tickets; the rest were offering to pay anything from 600 to 1000 dollars for a seat!

They got an ecstatic reaction from a predominantly early-teen female crowd. 'This has to be the loudest audience we've ever had,' Harry said into the microphone, making them even louder.

The group, who were stylishly decked out in blazers, skinny jeans and matching trainers, wowed the crowds with tracks 'Na Na Na' and 'Stand Up', before paying tribute to their first stabs at being a boyband by playing acoustically some of the covers they had first rehearsed together, such as 'Torn' and Kings of Leon's 'Use Somebody'. Then, after broadcasting a handful of Twitter dedications, and a quick costume change, they belted out a few more hits, including 'Everything About You' and 'What Makes You Beautiful'.

The *Herald Sun* said: 'The five boys are already consummate professionals at working the crowd, rewarding the front rows with a smile or a point. They stand out from the rest of the pop crowd by keeping their choreography to simple stage blocking rather than intensive dance sections. But the real key to their appeal is that One Direction is always up.'

Much to the delight of women everywhere, Niall tweeted a series of arty black-and-white pictures of Harry in his Tommy Hilfiger boxer shorts backstage. 'As we promised here is . . . #harryinhispants,' he wrote. In one, Harry appeared to be shaving his legs before putting the razor in Liam's face.

Perhaps the high jinks could have had something to do with people comparing Harry to Susan Boyle. The joke started when Louis likened Harry's doll to the BGT star and fans began mocking him for his bouffant hair!

The tour was taking its toll and the boys were exhausted and missing home but Anne said that, despite the time difference, Harry always made sure he contacted her five times a day to let her know he was OK. She told *Heat*: 'When there's a time difference, he tends to text saying, "I love you, Mum," or "I miss you". He's still my little boy . . . He gives the best hugs ever.'

She was also quick to dispel rumours that he was in a relationship. 'He'll make a nice boyfriend when he's ready. He's very sensitive and isn't a Jack the Lad. At the moment he doesn't want to tie himself down. He had one or two girlfriends when he was younger, but no one very special. I'd love Harry to have a family one day, and he'd love one, too. He'd make a fantastic dad. He's also a very romantic guy.' It seems Harry really would like to be a dad – he has already planned to call his first daughter Darcey!

Harry's dad, Des, commented that it is very hard for him to have a relationship because they are always so busy – but he had warned him not to get a girl pregnant, although he did also say that he reckoned Harry would take fatherhood in his stride.

From Sydney they travelled to Melbourne, where they performed at the Hisense Arena on 16 April. Again the venue was packed with their fans – the show had sold out in just three minutes – but there was one special guest dancing along in the VIP area: Dannii Minogue, who had judged them on *The X Factor*. Afterwards she met up with the boys and told them how proud she was of them, and how seeing them in her hometown with hordes of fans screaming their names was a really special moment for her. Many loyal girls who had missed out on tickets camped outside to see if they could hear murmurs of the gig.

They showed up at the Logie Awards for a special per-formance for the prizewinners prior to the red carpet. After a number of banners with sexually explicit words were seen in Sydney, officials checked all the fans' posters as they arrived. The group also presented an award.

As they walked the red carpet, by now complete profes-sionals, Liam said: 'It's massively great to be in Australia. We're having a great time here, we even learnt to surf as well. But the only downside is that we don't really know any-body.'

Harry then quipped: 'So we thought, What better way for us to meet people that we would get on with than by pre-senting the "Most Popular Female Talent award"?'

From there, they travelled to Brisbane, where they visited the Lone Pine Koala Sanctuary and Harry took a picture of himself with a new furry friend called Kat. A million hearts melted, with fans commenting that they couldn't decide who was cuter. Harry posted the snap on Twitter, simply writing 'Koala!'

However, Kat wasn't quite as cuddly as he thought – she pooed on his grey t-shirt and then clung on as he tried to put her back down. A member of staff had to prise her off him! Afterwards Liam said they were concerned that they could have picked up chlamydia, which 8 per cent of koalas are infected with. Regardless, the boys couldn't believe that they were having so many wonderful experiences and trav-elling to so many places and they tried to pack as much into their time as they could.

Next stop was New Zealand, where they stayed at the five-star Langham Auckland hotel. The boys and their entourage had booked out the top two floors of the hotel. Many fans waited outside hoping to see them and 1D waved from the windows.

Before their work commitments, they took some time out and Louis and Liam were brave enough to bungee jump from the Sky Tower, following in the footsteps of David

Beckham, Justin Bieber and Katy Perry, who have all leapt from the tower. Harry didn't take part – maybe because he wasn't feeling too adventurous. He decided to keep his feet firmly on the ground and instead hung out with Lux, their stylist Lou's baby girl.

Louis and Liam then joined Harry, Zayn and Niall at Eden Park for a Kiwis–Kangaroos rugby league game. As mass hysteria followed wherever the boys went, police joined forces with ambulance and security staff to make sure fans were taken care of. They dubbed it Operation One Direction. Thousands of girls turned up at the TV station where they were due to be interviewed and there were fears of crushing.

They played two shows at the city's Trusts Stadium, where 10,000 tickets sold out in just under ten minutes. No cameras were allowed inside the show but fans described the first gig as 'life-changing' and 'amazing'. This would probably be how Harry and the boys would describe their time in Australia and New Zealand too. The kind of following they had managed to get in such a short space of time was mind-blowing. They really had taken over the world.

While they were touring New Zealand Harry reportedly hooked up with an Auckland-based model, Emma Ostilly, who was also eighteen at the time. It is believed that they first met when the group filmed the video to 'Gotta Be You', which was shot in New York where Emma lives and works. As soon as he arrived in the country Harry tracked her down as he knew she was at home.

The pair hung out at Grey Lynn's Gypsy Tea Room, then were pictured kissing outside Emma's flat at 1.20 a.m. An onlooker told the *Daily Mirror*: 'They were enjoying themselves, laughing and joking together. They seemed very happy and relaxed and you could tell they have a history together. The pictures show they are still close.'

Emma also snuck into the boys' hotel the following night and the group went to a few bars before being driven back by Harry's driver in the early hours of the morning.

When he was asked if he was dating a girl from New Zealand, he replied: 'No she's not a New Zealander, she's just a friend,' before Liam cut in: 'She's not his girlfriend either.'

'No . . . She's working over here,' Harry added. 'I prefer not to talk about her.'

But with the evidence of them kissing stacked up against the pair, it later emerged that Emma had a boyfriend, Sean Gallagher, who she had been dating for about a year. He was in the navy and was away with work.

A friend of the couple, Conor Mahoney, who reportedly went to school with Emma, told *Now* magazine: 'Sean was really hurt. They've talked it over and decided they'll both move on from it. I'm not sure how Sean found out – whether she told him or he heard it in the news. But they're still together and working through it.'

For their final stop, they went to Wellington, arriving at noon the following day. Around 300 screaming teenage girls spent several hours singing and chanting outside the Inter-

Continental hotel in central Wellington where the band was staying, in the hope of catching a peep of one of them. Members of the band periodically appeared at a hotel window, sending the crowd into a frenzy.

Their last concert in New Zealand was at the St James Theatre and they finished off with a bit of a surprise – they wore each other's costumes during the gig's opening track. The boys had worn the same clothes for the first song of the Up All Night tour for pretty much every single show, and for their tour with Big Time Rush in North America too. So they decided to switch things up by putting on each other's outfits. Zayn wore Liam's checked shirt, Niall put on Louis' striped tee, Louis wore Harry's t-shirt and blazer, Harry put on Niall's red polo and Liam rocked Zayn's varsity jacket.

They may only have been out of the country for a few months but, judging by the reception at Heathrow Airport, it felt like a year for the British fans who were there screaming their names to welcome them back on to home turf. Laden down with bags of duty-free, they hugged the waiting girls and vowed to sleep for a year. The boys were given six weeks off to recover from their massive trip and they needed it – they were shattered.

Arriving back home in Cheshire, Harry slept for most of the day before watching some Jeremy Kyle. As fans waited outside his mum's house, he emerged and showed off his new car – a black Audi R8 Coupé with grey panels. Dressed in a beige sheepskin jacket over a white hoodie, a white t-shirt and black jeans, he climbed inside and went to pick up his sister from the train station. He also gave a lift to one of his friends who had a broken leg. Unfortunately for him, his mum doesn't have a garage at the family home, so he was forced to park his new motor outside on the driveway or on a side road. A big fan of flashy cars, he has also previously been seen test-driving a vintage red Jaguar E-Type roadster and a Porsche 911 Sport Classic.

Talking about his love of vintage cars in *OK!* magazine, Harry said that a friend's dad was a classic car dealer and that he'd had a lot of fun choosing between the many beautiful vehicles he could now afford. Viewing them as a sound investment he acknowledged: 'If I didn't have fun with it, I'd just end up a bitter old man ... I think if you invest in the right things, cars can be as safe as property.'

Harry was delighted to be back at home and able to help his parents. Harry said if his mum has had a bad day, he will run her a bath and cook dinner; his speciality is apparently Mexican food. Even though he tried to keep everything as normal as possible, getting to and from his house was becoming increasingly difficult. The situation had become so bad that he could no longer park in his own drive as this would alert fans that he was home and they would then mob his house. To get around this Harry and Will would come up with elaborate ways of sneaking Harry out – this included hiding him under a pile of coats in the footwell. But, never wanting to miss the chance for a practical joke, Will would sometimes tell Harry it was safe to come out but actually still be in full view of the fans who would then chase them down the street.

During his time off he was seen with a number of friends, including pretty blonde Ellis Calcutt, who is one of his good friends. They were papped together in Manchester giggling in a coffee shop before he took her for a spin in his new wheels.

After Directioners got wind of the pics and started speculating whether the two were an item, she took to Twitter to deny there was anything between them. She said: 'Wow, you people are sooo quick to make up rumours! Me & Harry went for coffee together as we haven't seen each other since last year! We're only good friends and have been since high school. I have a lovely boyfriend called Phil so you can stop spreading rumours about me and Harry dating each other because we absolutely are not!'

However, not everyone in Holmes Chapel was so friendly towards Harry. One of the downsides of such quick success was the people who were jealous even though, like the rest of the band, he has always stayed very grounded. Will told *The People* that some of the local lads called him a 'dickhead' and a 't***'.

'It really upsets Harry because he's a sensitive guy. He doesn't understand it either. People call him a dickhead and refer to him as that t***. More recently he's had abuse on network sites and chatrooms.'

Will said the singer has learned to ignore the nasty comments by rising above it. 'He's had quite a few tweets and comments posted on Facebook and on the Internet from people calling him names. He doesn't read the messages any more. He just ignores them now. It gets him down and when he comes back to see his family he just likes to keep out of the way of some people because of what they've said.'

Concerned fans took to Twitter after the article was published but Anne was quick to reassure them that her son was fine. She wrote: 'Harry is fine. Please don't fret :)'.

In May they headed back to Sweden and then on to LA to start recording more tracks for their second album. Niall had previously said they hoped to create a new album every year to eighteen months. They knew they need to keep evolving as a group and doing new things to keep their fans interested.

The crack team of songwriters was busy behind the scenes. Many remained anonymous, however, McFly frontman Tom Fletcher confirmed that he would be writing a song for the album, and later Ed Sheeran – who the boys describe as 'the sixth member of the band' – said they would be using two of his songs.

Harry said that the band were helping with the songwriting. He told *The Sun*: 'We're always writing on the road and in hotels and airports. We don't ever want our music to sound like a 40-year-old man in an office has written it and given it to us to perform.'

During a different interview, he said he was worried about how their second album would go down: 'Yeah I think we are worried that it's going to be game over. Everyone's said that second albums are the hardest, so before we started recording we were a bit nervous.' Then he added: 'But I think we had a little bit more experience this time, we had a bit more input and I think we've got better songs this time so the album should be better.'

Swedish producer and songwriter Carl Falk, who worked with them on 'What Makes You Beautiful', played a massive part and said he wanted to get the boys' personalities into the music. He also said he felt Swedish music was working for them.

'Swedes have been making great pop songs since ABBA. We love melodies and nice chord changes. That fits the market right now. Melody is back, pop is back and young girls want their pop idols again.'

Later in the year, the boys' collaboration with Ed Sheeran took place in a secret location in Buckinghamshire. The boys were photographed taking time out of recording with a game of football, which Harry says that, considering his knowledge of the game (he is a big fan of Manchester United) he's not very good at. Afterwards he relaxed on one of the outdoor sofas.

Ed had previously spoken of his good friendship with Harry, telling Xfm: 'They're really cool guys. Harry's a lad – I was with him last night actually. Being in music you're quite segregated from everyone and you're always busy doing promo. When you're on the same promo run as someone or in the same kind of situation as someone you grow quite close, friendship-wise. He's a very cool guy.'

Ed also said he had seen Harry in the nude one day on the band's tour bus. 'I turned around and Harry was stripped off and completely naked, just sitting there laughing,' he told Australia's 2Day FM. When he was asked if Harry was well endowed, Ed replied: 'He's packing heat, yeah. He's packing heat.'

Harry has also spoken about his respect for Ed, saying: 'It's so nice to have someone of a similar age going through the same sort of thing. So obviously our two circumstances are very different – but very similar at the same time. So it's nice.'

At the end of May 1D started back on their Up All Night tour in the US and Barack Obama's daughter Malia was seen in the crowd at the show in Fairfax, Virginia, which is just 20 miles from Washington's White House.

In Camden, New Jersey, Harry tweeted a picture of him with Blink-182 drummer Travis Barker – and it seems like he might have been inspired to live a little more on the wild side.

'Everyone was saying we weren't very rock 'n' roll,' Harry explained. 'I thought I'd throw a TV out of the Winnebago window.' However it didn't exactly go to plan: not only did it not smash, it didn't even have a scratch on it!

Harry insists he would never go crazy like some pop stars and his antics are just like any other teenager. He told *OK!* magazine: 'I can see how you can get dragged into bad stuff. But I've got good friends around me, good family. I've got my head screwed on. I'm doing stuff that every other 18-year-old lad is doing but it is getting written about.'

While they were in the States Harry wanted an all-American smile, so booked himself in for some teeth whitening, while Zayn had a manicure. Harry, who is never afraid of laughing at himself, posted a picture, which was taken while he was in the dentist's chair with goggles on and his mouth held open with a special contraption. He accompanied it with the caption: 'Bit of manly pampering.'

When they went to Canada to perform in Toronto, they took time out to visit Niagara Falls and went on a Maid of the Mist boat ride, where they were seen wearing bright blue ponchos to protect themselves from the spray. The band were also spotted making a pit stop at a local branch of Taco Bell and went on the Cave of the Winds tour – a ride in a lift down into the gorge of the falls. It was a fairly gentle ride, as Harry's biggest fear is roller coasters. They also went to the Mirror Maze at the Crystal Caves.

While in Chicago, Harry fell victim to Liam and Zayn, who ripped off his shirt during a performance of 'What Makes You Beautiful'. As he sang his solo part, they grabbed him, pulling his white shirt off and revealing his chest and abs. He laughed it off and the fans went wild – and, of course, thanked the boys on Twitter.

The pranks continued: in Mexico City, Niall and Louis started play-fighting while Harry looked on. Louis pretended to hit the Irish singer in the face and he fell to the ground. While they were in Mexico, they stayed at the Four Seasons hotel and Harry published a picture of the breathtaking view from his room via Instagram.

In Houston, Harry messed around by pretending to kiss Niall during the show, tapping him on the shoulder then appearing to lean in. The duo then earned themselves the nickname 'Narry' after the apparent act of bromance. Referring to the other three singers' current girlfriends, one Twitter user wrote: 'Liam and Danielle, Louis and Eleanor, Zayn and Perrie and then we have Niall and Harry... #Narry!'

Then during one gig, Louis and Harry changed the words of 'Gotta Be You' to 'big brown poo'. They were seen plotting just before Harry belted it out to the appreciative audience.

However, Zayn and Louis managed an even better prank with the help of Nickelodeon. Just before they went on stage for an interview, there was a crisis when a producer pretended she was about to have a baby; it was actually an actress with a prosthetic bump. As she wailed, the boys moved the chairs around and called for her husband, with Zayn and Louis increasing the other three's panic. Harry, in particular, looked really worried, especially as the boys appeared to be on their own in the building with her. He started shouting: 'Why is no one here? Can somebody help us?!'

Moments later, the actress revealed the prank to the One Direction trio and the crowd went wild, while Harry fell to the floor and had to be consoled. He managed to save face by saying that he was thinking about how much press 1D would get for helping to deliver a baby!

It seems that as momentum around the band and its good-looking members grew, everyone wanted to meet Harry, and teenage model Alli Simpson was no exception, posting a picture of them on her Twitter page after interviewing the group for Radio Disney, a few days after seeing them in concert.

And while she was more than satisfied with simply posing for a happy snap with Harry, the 18-year-old has admitted she had to fight off older women, who are much more confident when they meet him.

'The fans sometimes get very graphic and there are a few mums that hit on us,' Harry revealed.

Louis added: 'Ask Harry – they just go for it. They will grab and pinch and it gets quite tricky.'

They had another handful of concerts in the US and finished the tour on 1 July in Florida, where they showed their appreciation by peeling off their bow ties and waistcoats and throwing them into the audience.

After a gruelling seven months, and sixty performances, you would think that a rest would be in order, but they had to complete the recording of their second album – and Niall told MTV News that July and August would be spent getting it finished. They were exhausted but it was such a whirlwind they knew they had to keep running with it.

Talking about the title of the album, *Take Me Home*, Niall

said: 'We thought about it for a while. Because we all do a lot of travelling around the world and we get to see a lot of cool places, but the main thing is there's no place like home. It's always kind of nice to go home.'

They arrived back in the UK in July to another brilliant reception from fans at Heathrow. Despite being bleary-eyed after the long flight, Harry signed autographs and had pictures taken with the girls who had been waiting. He was happy to be back on British soil; his life felt slightly out of control but in a really good way, and British 1D fans were delighted to have their boys back.

CHAPTER NINE

'For me the Olympics literally can't be topped'

Home to stars including Kate Moss, Sadie Frost, Daniel Craig and Daisy Lowe, Primrose Hill is located on the north side of Regent's Park and has a villagey feel with independent shops, cosy cafés and uber-cool pubs. After their Up All Night tour had finished, Harry started to look for a new home in the area on the advice of his friend Nick Grimshaw, who owns a studio flat there. Grimmy once said in an interview with *ES* magazine: 'If a Disney movie were set in London, it would look like Primrose Hill.'

At the end of July Harry was spotted house-hunting, alongside his blonde hairdresser and One Direction make-up artist Lou Teasdale, who grew up in the same town as Harry. The boys are all good friends with Lou, who they describe as an older-sister figure. While on tour, Harry had taken to Twitter to tease her, writing: 'According to @louteasdale dolphins are like "Swimming cows". Wow.'

Lou had also posted a snap of her adorable little girl and Harry playing on the laptop together, with the words, 'Harry and Lux doin some spreadsheets makin some deals.' Harry also tweeted a message revealing he was having a good day watching *Pingu* with the cute tot. The message to Lou read: '@louteasdale Lux is "buzzing"' watching Pingu.' Aww!

As he walked around the celebrity enclave with Lou and an estate agent, Harry – who appeared to be in good spirits – was wearing black skinny jeans, white Converse trainers and a grey t-shirt with the word 'Love' emblazoned on the pocket.

The estate agent, who cheekily asked Harry for an autograph, showed them a £2-million luxury mews house. However, an insider said 'it wasn't for him' and he continued on his search. A few days later Liam was spotted looking at a two-bedroom, 1,400 sq ft home that was on the same street, worth £1.35 million. He was clearly also hoping to invest his new-found fortune in bricks and mortar.

Two months later, in September, it was revealed that Harry had purchased a £3-million, 2,300 sq ft pad in the area with four bedrooms, three bathrooms, several living areas and a gorgeous, landscaped south-west-facing garden, equipped with Ibiza-style loungers. It was enormous compared to his previous home and insiders said it was 'the perfect party pad'. It has high walls – and therefore plenty of privacy, as fans and photographers can't watch his every move. Importantly, there are also four off-road spaces for cars, as well as a James Bond-style double car-lift.

Later, it emerged that he had splashed out £100,000 on pictures of Kate Moss and Rihanna by Banksy and female graffiti artist Bambi to adorn the walls. Art trader Lenny Villa told the *Mail on Sunday*: 'We've had a call from a dealer who says Harry is looking for investment art, but modern and funky. We're sending him Bambi's painting of Rihanna and a Banksy print of Kate Moss. Harry knows Robbie Williams and Brad Pitt both own a Bambi.'

Harry has previously said that he's not an art expert but if he sees a piece that he's keen on he'll purchase it, and that one of his favourite artists is Tracey Emin.

He was also said to have got Kate Moss' furnishing contacts from her, along with details of her favourite shops and florists in the exclusive area.

After all that spending, it seems he still had money to burn and was seen wearing a £23,250 Audemars Piguet watch while running errands. The lavish timepiece is made up of 280 parts and 40 jewels, with an 18-carat pink gold clasping fold and a black hand-stitched crocodile strap. Other celeb fans include Jay-Z, who immortalised the watches in his track 'Paris', a collaboration with Kanye West.

However, Harry is never stupid with his money. He told *Fabulous* magazine: 'My dad's a financial adviser so that helps. He's always said to me, "for every £10 you make, say you spend £7 of it wisely, the other £3 it doesn't matter what you do."'

It seems Harry can't be pictured with any woman without them being linked and a couple of days after his initial house hunt, he was seen cosying up to *Made in Chelsea*'s Caggie Dunlop, who is five years his senior, at west London's Dorsia club. After partying for a few hours, the couple were seen speeding away towards Chelsea Harbour in Harry's Range Rover, but a 1D rep was forced to deny that they were in a relationship and said they are just friends.

Apparently Harry had started tweeting the pretty blonde reality star before the band had gone on tour in the US and Caggie had playfully responded to his advances, messaging 'do you want to come over'. She also wrote: 'I love harry styles'.

They finally met in the flesh a few weeks later at a party in east London and they really hit it off. Caggie then invited him to stay at her aunt's Chelsea flat but nothing happened because of the age difference.

Harry even palled up with Caggie's on/off boyfriend and co-star, Spencer Matthews. Spencer told *Heat* magazine: 'He was asking my advice on pocket hankies – he wanted to know whether to go for a square or a more voluminous option. Then we cut Caggie out of the loop and became mates. Caggie didn't like that!' He did admit that he had asked Caggie what Harry was like in bed, to which she responded, 'I don't know.' He added that he was sure she would have told him if something had happened, as why would she lie about it to her good friend?

Harry also made friends with *Made in Chelsea*'s Francis Boulle, who said he knew Harry 'pretty well' and had heard from a 'credible source' – not Caggie – that 'apparently he has a big penis'!

Unsurprisingly, even though it seems romance was never on the cards, Caggie went on to receive abuse on Twitter and Caggie's friend and *Made in Chelsea* co-star, Millie Mackintosh, said she had been 'freaked out' by the reaction of some fans. Millie told *Marie Claire* magazine: 'I'm not going to speak about it but when people are showing up outside your parents' house it's gone too far. Caggie is a fun-loving girl, I don't think she minded the attention too much but it does all get a bit too much.'

At one stage, Harry was also linked to blonde *Inbetweeners* actress Emily Atack, but later he told *The Sun* that they only met a couple of times and are friends and have never even kissed, even though she said they kept in touch.

During July, Harry headed back home to Holmes Chapel for a spot of Sunday lunch but he hadn't even pulled into the driveway before about twenty teens surrounded his car, so he was forced to get out and walk the remaining distance to the house. Two fans hugged each other because they were so excited to see him, while one chased him down the street.

Although he's never usually one to shy away from attention of the female variety, Harry looked a little perplexed by the crowd. On some days, he just wished he could be invisible and lead a normal life but he knew that the attention was a small price to pay for the success he was having. Casually dressed in indigo skinny jeans, a grey t-shirt, blue checked shirt and white Converse trainers, the teen looked every inch the star as he walked away from the group wearing dark sunglasses.

1D were now back in the studio recording new music but they found time to take a private flight in the specially named BA1D from London to Manchester with winners of a competition in aid of charity. The boys helped to raise £50,000 for Flying Start, British Airways' charity partnership with Comic Relief. Always game for a laugh, Harry couldn't resist taking a snap of himself wearing the pilot's hat.

He has always tried to do some charity work when he has time and another cause he helped was the Help Harry Help Others campaign, which was set up by Harry Moseley, a young boy who sadly died from an inoperable brain tumour in October 2011. He spent two years making special bracelets, raising thousands of pounds for others with cancer, and Harry S was seen sporting some in a video. He described the young man as 'an inspiration'.

Later in July they were rumoured to have indulged in a spot of pampering and apparently flew by private helicopter to the five-star Danesfield House hotel in Buckinghamshire, where they had the spa reserved specially for them. Apparently a bridal party were staying there and the boys invited them into the jacuzzi!

Their next gig was Radio City Live on 21 July at the Echo Arena Liverpool alongside Professor Green, Stooshe, Alyssa

Reid, Labrinth, Alexandra Burke, Rizzle Kicks, Tulisa, Taio Cruz and Will Young.

When they got to their dressing room, Harry tweeted a picture of markers and a blank canvas, which had been left out, and joked: 'I know we're young but I feel like colouring books in the dressing room is a little far.'

Backstage, they spoke to ITV and the radio team and Harry said how much he enjoys being back near his hometown. He also showed off his new tattoo – an 'A' on his forearm for his mum, Anne. Louis said he is going slightly deaf in his right ear, due to the blood-curdling screaming – the boys' managers have worked out that the crowd's screams at gigs when the group plays sometimes reach 104 decibels.

If they hadn't already clocked that they'd made it in the US, their huge impact stateside was cemented after they walked away with three awards at the Teen Choice Awards the following day. They won gongs for Choice Breakout Group, Choice Love Song for 'What Makes You Beautiful' and they beat groups such as Maroon 5, Coldplay, Gym Class Heroes and their rivals The Wanted to the prize for Choice Summer Music Star Group.

They weren't able to pick up the awards in person at the Gibson Amphitheatre in LA because they were back home in the UK to perform a string of dates, but they kept award-goers amused with a cute and funny A-Team-inspired video message in which they struggled to reassemble their surf-board trophy (while wearing protective goggles), with hammers, glue sticks, string and sticky tape after it had been chopped up to try and get it through the post. They didn't have much luck and it was clear Harry wouldn't be adding to his DIY skills with some Pritt Stick.

Getting on with the acceptance speech, at the end of the video Zayn stepped up to thank fans. 'It's a real honour to receive this award because we know it's voted for by the fans so a massive thank you to you guys – thanks for this,' he said.

Following on from Zayn's words, all the boys gave a big cheer and simultaneously said: 'Thank you Teen Choice.'

The Teen Choice Awards took place at the same time as the date they were due to play at Party in the Park at Temple Newsam in Leeds, a free concert for 70,000 local people. According to reports, the organisers of the event were so concerned about them being surrounded by fans that they were instructed to arrive separately, wearing animal costumes! They were also planning to leave their normal transport behind and come in ordinary cars to avoid attracting attention.

In the end, it all ran like clockwork as they performed 'One Thing', 'Up All Night' and 'What Makes You Beautiful'. Harry wore a blazer with a hanky sticking out of the top pocket – its exact dimensions perhaps dictated by *Made in Chelsea*'s Spencer Matthews – and Zayn was able to spend more time with his girlfriend, Perrie Edwards.

A few days later Harry was seen on a lads' night out with JLS singer Aston Merrygold and Olly Murs at The Rose Club in London. Olly was at a great point in his career. The Essex singer is another good example of the fact that not winning *The X Factor* doesn't necessarily mean you won't be destined for chart success. After coming second in the 2009 series of the programme behind Joe McElderry, his debut single 'Please Don't Let Me Go' went to No. 1 and his self-titled album had the highest-selling week one sales for 2010, and eventually went double platinum. He went on to open 1D's Toronto gig in May. More successes followed and he had obviously also forged a good TV career after hosting the previous series of *The Xtra Factor* alongside Caroline Flack.

X Factor Series Five runners-up, Aston and the JLS boys were also flying high, landing No. 1 after No. 1, awards aplenty and selling over 10 million albums. Two years ahead of 1D, they have also had a number of sell-out tours.

As the trio hit the tiles, 24-year-old Aston tweeted: 'Smurf, Styles and Merrygold 1st team night out!! Let's get on it!! @ollyofficial @Harry_Styles BOSH Ax'. The guys arrived separately but Harry, looking every inch the star, was accompanied by a large entourage, which consisted of some of his management team and friends. He was quite reluctant to be photographed and only stayed a short while before heading with his friends to Jalouse, where he partied until 3.30 a.m.

Harry is quite good friends with all the JLS boys. Back in May he was spotted hugging Marvin Humes at Heathrow Airport. Harry was on his way back to LA and Marvin was en route to his stag do in Las Vegas, prior to his wedding to The Saturdays singer Rochelle Wiseman. As usual Harry looked gorgeous in tight skinny-leg jeans, a plain white t-shirt and high-collared jacket.

Harry had previously spoken about how he went to a party at Marvin's house with Niall and had a dodgy tummy. He told *We Love Pop* magazine: 'I fell asleep in his dog bed and I was sick in the night. It went everywhere. I think it was some bad chicken.'

A couple of weeks later, Harry was partying with Aston and Olly again at Marvin and Rochelle's wedding at Blenheim Palace in Oxfordshire, where Olly was rumoured to be performing. The intimate ceremony, watched by other celeb guests including Girls Aloud star Nicola Roberts, Tulisa Contostavlos and Alexandra Burke, was followed by a lavish reception. Rochelle's bandmates Mollie King, Vanessa White, Frankie Sandford and Una Healy were bridesmaids and the other JLS boys Aston, J.B. Gill and Oritsé Williams were on hand to support the groom. After the reception, a crowd headed back for more drinks at the nearby Feathers Hotel, where Harry was staying, along with Liam and Niall, who had also been invited.

Harry was pictured with Una, who was helping him home. He had unbuttoned his shirt and held his suit jacket in his hand, presumably taking it off earlier in the evening as the partygoers danced the night away. The pair appeared to be sharing a joke and were joined by Una's husband, rugby star Ben Foden.

DJ Pierzchalski tweeted: 'Drunk with @Harry_Styles #wedding', and later added: 'Sleep time 2 beds in my room

@Harry_Styles is sleeping! He got work tomorrow nyt-people.'

The boys congratulated the couple again on Twitter and the wedding donation website, where Marvin and Rochelle had generously asked guests to contribute to Marie Curie Cancer Care rather than give wedding presents. Harry wrote 'Congratulations! I hope you have a long and happy marriage. Love Harry x'.

Clearly on a high from the night before, Harry was walking around Oxford the next day in skinny jeans, dark glasses and a grey t-shirt emblazoned with the word 'lover' when he saw another bride, a member of the public. He stopped to congratulate her and gave her a kiss on the cheek. What a gent!

A few weeks later Rochelle tweeted a hilarious picture of her and Harry, along with Tulisa, Wretch 32, Reggie Yates and his stylist brother Cobbie, all packed into a photo booth.

Harry was certainly playing hard but he was also working hard and 1D joined the prestigious list of performers to play at the closing ceremony for the Olympics in front of billions of people around the world. Following performances from the Spice Girls, Emeli Sandé, Blur and Madness, the boys sang 'What Makes You Beautiful' on the flat top of an extended lorry. The curly-haired singer wore a dark suit, a blue shirt and white Converse trainers as he sang centre stage among the other four. The atmosphere was electric and Harry later said it was the best moment of his year. It would be a defining moment of their lives.

'For me the Olympics literally can't be topped,' he said to *Billboard*. 'Just the feeling of being in that room, all our families were there. The whole feeling was unbelievable.'

The boys then played at V Festival in Chelmsford, where they stayed in a tube-tent, which looked fun, although Niall revealed it got 'quite sweaty'. While Liam, Louis and Niall relaxed in the Virgin Media Louder Lounge, where some of music's biggest stars go to mingle and enjoy the free food and drink, Harry stuck to the exclusive Mahiki area backstage, alongside Olly Murs and Jessie J. And after they were spotted in the VIP areas by hordes of screaming fans, the boys were forced to retreat back to their communal tent. Liam, who was with his girlfriend Danielle, was the only one who stayed to mix with everyone.

At the beginning of September 1D were back in LA for the MTV Video Music Awards. The boys were seen greeting fans outside their hotel, on their way to rehearsals the day before the big event.

Harry told MTV News: 'I think people should expect a massive show from the VMAs this year. If you look at the people performing there are some massive, massive stars.' He added: 'It should be a great show, and we can't wait to perform. It's our first time so it should be fun.'

The *X Factor* stars picked up their first-ever MTV Video Music Award (VMA) just before the event officially started when the promo for hit track 'What Makes You Beautiful' was voted Most Share-Worthy Video by fans.

Their night got even better when the quintet – who also

performed 'One Thing' at the ceremony – went on to win Best New Artist and Best Pop Video for 'What Makes You Beautiful'.

However, it was probably Katy Perry who gave them the biggest thrill of the night, kissing each band member in turn as they collected the Best Pop Video prize. This affectionate act sent Twitter into meltdown mode.

'Harry kissing Katy Perry, re-tweet if you slammed your head into a mirror,' one fan tweeted.

'If you're hating on Katy Perry over one little kiss with Niall and Harry, then I will slit your throat,' another threatened.

However, the boys ignored the Twitter trolls and Niall said: 'Thank you so much! We have grown up watching this show and to collect one of these [awards] straight away is incredible.'

Simon Cowell tweeted the group saying: 'Congratulations 1D. I'm very proud of you. Celebrate!'

'This has been unbelievable,' Harry said backstage. 'This was our favourite performance we've ever done. For us to be here in the first place is amazing, and to perform and win a Moonman is amazing.'

They were getting used to going back and forwards across the globe by now and on 20 September they headlined the iTunes Festival, their first UK gig for nine months. The girls went crazy as a 60-second countdown appeared on giant screens either side of the stage at Camden's Roundhouse. They kicked the performance off with 'Na Na Na', followed by 'I Wish', when someone threw a bra on to the stage. Louis told their screaming fans: 'We have spent time outside of the UK and it is incredible to be back in London.'

They also performed 'One Thing', 'What Makes You Beautiful' and covers, including The Zutons' 'Valerie', The Black Eyed Peas' 'I Gotta Feeling' and Natalie Imbruglia's 'Torn', which Harry and Liam sang together. Nick Grimshaw and fellow BBC DJ and partner in crime Annie Mac, who were presenting TV coverage of the gig, asked the five-piece to describe each other in one word. Zayn echoed the feelings of the crowd when he labelled Harry as 'sexy'. Harry also said he'd like to change his name to Dave and that he misses roast dinners most when he's away. They did impressions of each other and performed the rap from *The Fresh Prince of Bel-Air*, much to the amusement of the delighted crowd.

Following the performance, they released their new single, 'Live While We're Young', on 28 September as the lead single from the second album, *Take Me Home*. They had filmed the video during the August Bank Holiday weekend on location in Tunbridge Wells. They were directed by Vaughan Arnell, who had worked with them on 'One Thing' and had previously helmed videos for Robbie Williams and the Spice Girls.

The group messed around on the bizarre set, which included a paddling pool, teepee, trampoline, hay bales and an inflatable banana. After diving in the paddling pool, Harry was left virtually topless under a soaked-through t-shirt. He wrote: 'And that's the video for Live While We're Young done. Amazing crew, amazing people.'

The video was leaked on the Internet a week before release and the same day, it was officially published on 1D's Vevo channel on YouTube because of the leak. They said: 'We wanted our fans to see the video and hear the single in the proper way so we've moved the premiere to tonight. We're really excited about LWWY, we've worked really hard on it and we can't wait for everyone to see and hear it later today!'

It went on to break the Vevo record for having the most views in a 24-hour period with 8.24 million, beating Justin Bieber's previous record for 'Boyfriend', although he got back this record a few weeks later.

The song was written by the team behind 'What Makes You Beautiful' and 'One Thing' – Rami Yacoub, Carl Falk and Savan Kotecha – and was another uptempo bubblegum pop offering, but unusually Zayn took the lead vocals. The critics gave it mixed reviews. Mikael Wood of the *Los Angeles Times* said it was a 'characteristically peppy piece of high-gloss party pop', *The Huffington Post* called it a 'poppy, energetic happy-go-lucky track', and 4Music labelled it 'insanely catchy'. However, some critics commented that the song's lyrics were a euphemism for sex and *HitFix*'s Melina Newman called the lyrics 'blatant', 'unwieldy' and 'uncouth'.

She argued that the more racy lyrics and subtext of their new songs couldn't possibly go over their 'tween audience's head'. She went on to say that the change in style was inevitable as the young boys turned into men.

Savan later defended the choice of words and said to *Sugarscape*: 'The whole idea is that you have that nostalgic night out, so people who are older can listen to it too. None of us are naive enough not to know what kids do. It's important not to patronize the youth of today, we're not gonna be writing about "oh let's just hold hands for a while" you know? They need their music to connect. A lot of songs are about sex and you have to be realistic about it.'

It peaked in the top ten in almost every country where it charted and entered the US *Billboard* chart at No. 3, the highest ever by a UK group in the chart's 54-year history. It was also the second-highest debut of any UK act, only outplaced by Elton John's 'Candle in the Wind', which went straight in at No. 1 in 1997.

The new single also featured in a hugely exciting new venture for the boys promoting Pepsi. The deal, reportedly worth a massive £11 million, saw them following in the footsteps of David Beckham, Britney Spears, the Spice Girls and Michael Jackson. The boys filmed the campaign in New Orleans alongside some big American football stars.

They flew to Tampa before boarding a private jet, laid on by Pepsi, which took them to New Orleans. There they met quarterback Drew Brees, who taught them the ropes of American football. They were forced to keep quiet about their whereabouts during this time so it was a complete surprise.

Harry takes a starring role in the commercial, which shows him having an argument with Drew about who is going to have the last Pepsi. Eventually Drew joins the band as their sixth member, singing the chorus of 'Live While We're Young' out of tune. Harry said: 'Pepsi is such a huge company that we've seen since we were little so to have the opportunity to work with them to do a commercial is good fun.'

The first time they performed the song to a UK audience they were suspended on an incredible floating plinth, above the audience at the BBC Radio 1 Teen Awards on 7 October at Wembley Arena, sending the crowd into a frenzy. They picked up a clean sweep of awards, landing Best British Single for 'One Thing', Best British Album for *Up All Night* and Best British Music Act. Afterwards Harry wrote on Twitter: 'Thank you again to BBC R1 for having us … Thank you everyone who voted! So happy to win!'

The day before he had co-presented a show on Radio 1 with Nick Grimshaw in honour of the event. During their time on air, Harry and Grimmy, who were standing in for Vernon Kaye, rebranded the show *Lads FM*. They discussed Harry's secret trips to Radio 1 during Grimmy's late-night shows, the length of the 1D star's toenails – he said he thought it was 3 mm before bursting into laughter about where he thought the question was initially going – and their 10-year age gap.

Grimmy was tested when he said he couldn't differentiate

Harry's vocals from the rest of the 1D members. After playing six clips from the album, Harry got him to try to identify each one and the presenter failed miserably.

And the good pals – who also treated listeners to a couple of photo-booth snaps – went down a storm with Directioners. One said: 'Harry and Grimmy are the perfect couple . . . love them.' Another suggested they consider their own show: 'I could listen to Harry and Grimmy ALL DAY!!!! They should do a podcasts week even if they don't have their own radio show @r1breakfast'.

CHAPTER TEN

'At the moment it appears I have, like 7000 girlfriends'

At the beginning of August Harry caused a stir once again – this time for leaving the exclusive Olympic VIP club at Omega House with pretty young model Cara Delevingne. The pair hopped into Harry's black Range Rover at 1 a.m. and sped away under the cover of darkness. Two weeks before that they had apparently been seen sunbathing by the pool on the roof of exclusive private members' club Shoreditch House. According to reports, they had met earlier in the summer at super-cool nightclub Le Baron, where they were introduced by Nick Grimshaw and Pixie Geldof, and had been texting one another ever since.

Cara, who is a statuesque 5 ft 9 in tall, has been touted as the fashion world's 'next big thing' and has modelled for everyone from Chanel to Stella McCartney, gracing glossy magazine covers and the catwalk. Described by *Vogue* as the star face of the season, she is tall and blonde with a tiny waist and surprisingly thick eyebrows. She once joked: 'They are their own beasts. I can't tame them.'

Cara's older sister, Poppy, had previously admitted to having a crush on Harry, telling *Grazia* magazine: 'I want to sit on Harry Styles' lap. I have a total crush on him. He walked past me at the Aquascutum show recently and I was salivating. I like his curly hair and he looks like a little cherub.'

There were reports that he was asked to sing at Cara's twentieth birthday party, which was being jointly organised by Cara and Poppy.

A couple of weeks after they were first seen together at Omega House, Cara was asked about Harry at the Topshop show at London Fashion Week and coyly replied: 'I've heard this thing. I'm not going to answer this question. I keep my private life private and that's all I'm going to say.'

The supermodel also responded to the inevitable barrage of questions from fans on Twitter. One said: 'sorry to inform you, but you look like a dude :/ #NoHate #TellingTheTruth'. Cara replied: 'hahaha well it seems to have worked well for me.'

Another fan added, 'i dont like you sorry' to which the model retorted, 'fair enough, but you don't really know me and then you apologize after? Funny'. Finally, she responded to questions about whether the rumours were true by saying, 'please just stop guessing, you don't need to know.' However, later she teased Directioners by telling singer Azealia Banks that she had a 'crush', writing: '@azealia-banks: I have a crush . . . Crushes are exciting . . . !!!!'

She thanked some of the public for the support with a pretty heavy hint that she was in love, penning: 'I want to say thank you guys to everyone who is sticking up for me and also how much I appreciate the kind words. LOVE YOU GUYS', adding: 'Everyone just stop hating on each other, LOVE IS IN THE AIR!'

Harry also did little to dispel the rumours they were dating when he went to see her a few days later as she graced the catwalk at the Burberry show in Kensington Gardens. He took to the hailed front row, along with Dita Von Teese, Dev Patel, Andy Murray and his girlfriend Kim Sears, Tali Lennox, Anna Wintour and Victoria Pendleton.

When ITN asked him what he thought of Cara's appearance, he replied: 'She was great, she did a good job. She looked amazing.' Then he was caught congratulating her on camera with a huge hug and kiss.

Commenting on the fashion house, Harry, who was wearing a white shirt and fitted grey jacket, said: 'The show was great. I thought the collection was really amazing. I've always been a fan of Burberry. The colours are nice and subtle, they aren't too much and it's easy to wear.'

And when he was asked what his favourite look on a girl is, he joked: 'Burberry. Whatever makes them feel most comfortable.' Cryptically, he also said he likes girls who wear coats!

He left the after-party early and went off with Pixie Geldof and some friends to Soho karaoke bar Lucky Voice, where Alexa Chung joined them. They arrived around midnight and the first song they put on was One Direction's 'What Makes You Beautiful'. An embarrassed Harry apparently avoided that choice but after a few vodka and cokes plucked up the courage to join in and sang Justin Bieber's 'Boyfriend'. More pals joined them, including Grimmy and designer Henry Holland. The group left in the early hours and sped off in Harry's car back to his house.

There was a huge amount of interest in Harry and Cara's blossoming romance. *The Sun* reported that Cara's management had warned her off dating Harry, saying he was the 'wrong image' for her and would damage her high-end jobs, while *Look* magazine claimed that he had already given her a key to his home.

However, Harry was staying non-committal once again and told *Now* magazine that many of his friends are mistaken for girlfriends.

'The thing is, I do have friends – and I'd say more than 90 per cent of the people I get linked to are my friends. At the moment it appears I have, like 7000 girlfriends. It's ridiculous. I think it's crazy. It does get in the way if I like someone. I'll say, "I like you," And they'll say, "But what about this and that?" I have to tell them it's not true. But it gets a bit tiring too.'

However, they appeared to be getting closer and days later Cara was seen with Harry and Grimmy at Mahiki in Mayfair, where they had gone to celebrate Rita Ora's first headline show at the Scala nightclub earlier in the night.

Harry and Grimmy had struck up quite a friendship with Rita and a few weeks earlier had been seen at G-A-Y for her album launch. She tweeted a picture of the trio saying: 'Thanks for coming my little fashionistas. Looking flyer than a mofo.' Harry describes her as 'very funny ... And she's hot.'

Fans were thrilled with the performance and took to Twitter, with one user saying: 'Rita Ora was amazing at G-A-Y tonight, however following the Harry Styles backstage food fight, we may need a cleaner!' He then posted a picture of sweets covering the floor in what was presumably the G-A-Y green room.

Perhaps they were no longer hungry – the duo had been seen earlier in the day grabbing a takeaway before their night out.

After a trip to LA a month later Harry returned two days after his bandmates – and people speculated that he had been spending time with rumoured girlfriend Cara, as she was in the States for New York Fashion Week. However, during the same week, viewers saw an episode of *The X Factor Australia* in which the boys were guest mentors on the show and Harry was linked to one of the contestants, Briden-Starr.

Harry appeared particularly taken when she performed

with her band, especially when she winked at him. Afterwards he said: 'I think I'm in love with her. I'm not even kidding. The one with the short blonde hair.' Louis then pointed out: 'It's 'cos she winked.'

Harry's friendship with Grimmy seemed to be getting stronger by the day and on 11 August Harry attended his twenty-eighth birthday bash at London's Groucho Club with Tulisa, Sadie Frost, Jaime Winstone and Kate Moss. According to *The Sun*, Kate made a beeline for Harry, telling him that her daughter Lila is a huge fan, and even sat on his knee for a picture to show her. They are now friends and Harry told *The Sun*: 'It's cool with people like Kate. I wouldn't say I was really great mates with her but it's weird for her to go, when I saw her at the Olympics, "Oh Harry come over". That's a bit weird.'

Caroline Flack was also there and it isn't known whether they spoke to each other inside the party but they left separately. Harry – who was wearing a grey denim jacket – chose to go home alongside a group of other women. It seems unavoidable that Harry and Caroline would bump into each other, having so many mutual friends, and a week or so later they were seen again at another pal's birthday party at the Sanctum Soho Hotel where they happily chatted.

A few days after Grimmy's birthday, Harry and the radio DJ were seen clowning around on Primrose Hill. Harry had brought a stretchy suit printed with muscles called a Muscle Morphsuit with him. After changing out of his three-quarter-length trousers and beanie hat, he put it on with hilarious effects. Grimmy was taking pictures on his mobile phone while Harry raced up and down.

Commenting on their close friendship, Harry said: 'We chatted a little bit and then we kept bumping into each other. Then we hung out a couple of times. We have the same sense of humour and we're from the same place. His brother's from where my dad lives. He's just so funny. You can hear that on the radio – he just makes me laugh a lot.'

In September Grimmy became the new host of the Radio 1 *Breakfast Show*, replacing Chris Moyles in a bid to attract younger listeners. Harry had appeared in advertising material for Nick's new show, with the singer supporting the Team Grimmy campaign. He called on fans and listeners to show their support for his friend by posting pics showing the hashtag #teamgrimmy on Twitter, with the singer also donning Grimmy's trademark slick quiff.

To mark his last late-night show, Harry joined Grimmy for some 'hip hop karaoke' and he and Example sang George Michael's 'Careless Whisper' very badly. Pixie Geldof, Annie Mac and Henry Holland were also seen at the BBC for the occasion but Harry didn't join them for drinks after the show and was seen driving away.

On his first day in the new job Grimmy pulled out his trump card – by waking Harry at 8 a.m., and promising to wake up one of the 1D team every day.

Nick said: 'The plan was to play One Direction's latest single. Then it was leaked and we were like, "Oh . . . but let's talk to them anyway! They really need the push, so they can start doing really well". I originally demanded to talk to them at 7.20 a.m. but their management said it was too early.'

In October he made a prank call to Harry live on air, while he was with Tulisa, playing Call or Delete, a simple game which involves pranking someone or losing their number from your phonebook for ever. When Harry was selected at random, Grimmy called him but before they got far into the conversation, Harry wised up and said: 'I'm on the radio, aren't I?'

Hilariously, Harry joined Grimmy one day and decided to play a joke on his stylist Caroline Watson while playing the game. After she picked up, Harry nonchalantly said to her: 'I was reading a magazine today and I saw this big article in the back and it was talking about men wearing tights. And, like, I was wondering because, erm, basically, whenever you've got me dressed, I don't know what it is, it just feels really comfortable, so I've been putting them under my jeans.'

He then joked he wanted 'crotchless ones' and that he had been 'stealing his sister's ones' and his stylist completely fell for it, telling him she would bring some with her to their next meeting.

Later Nick told *Heat* magazine that, despite the age difference, he doesn't feel protective of Harry.

He said: 'I don't feel protective – he's smart and savvy enough not to need a protector ... He's probably wiser and more clued up about things than me. He's conquered America and all that, and I'm like, "Let me tell you about the time I DJ'ed in Milton Keynes" . . . He's like, "I've just played Madison Square Garden, so I'm fine for advice, thanks".'

He added that most of their nights out together are spontaneous. But he did admit he was blown away by the attention Harry receives, calling it 'full-on'.

They also have a habit of wearing similar clothes. Grimmy was seen out in a distinctive orange raincoat that Harry wore on the cover of their single, 'Live While We're Young'. And a few weeks later he was pictured in the same grey jumper that Harry had been spotted in a few days earlier. However, the DJ was quick to say it was a coincidence, rather than them sharing closets. Grimmy told the journalist that he had spent hours agonising over whether or not to buy the orange coat – he couldn't decide whether it was absolutely hideous or really on trend. It had never crossed his mind, however, that his friend might have it too! He did admit that he borrowed the grey jumper from Harry, but added: 'we don't sit and raid each other's wardrobes and play swapsies.'

Hilariously, Grimmy was once mistaken for Harry's dad – a moment which he describes as a 'real low-point' – when they went shopping together at Selfridges in Manchester. Harry was trying on a jumper in the changing rooms when a shop assistant told Grimmy that he must be proud of his son. Apparently Harry was laughing hysterically – but promised he wouldn't tell anyone. Later Harry was mistaken for 2011 *X Factor* reject Frankie Cocozza, something that he wasn't highly impressed with.

However, their bromance has got people talking, and comedian Russell Howard spoke out about the age difference. 'I'd say I am a famous comedian, not a celebrity,' he told *The Sun*. 'Some people latch on to it and become friends with celebrities. It's so odd. The one that intrigues me is Nick Grimshaw hanging out with Harry Styles. Like Nick is my age and Harry is about eighteen and they play Frisbee together – it's rather weird. How have they become best buddies? I'd rather hang out with my mates and do gigs.'

Poor Harry often felt like his every relationship was analysed and poured over.

At the end of September, Harry was a guest at another celebrity wedding, that of James Corden to Julia Carey. Held at Babington House in Somerset, the star-studded guest list included Kylie Minogue, David Walliams, Jimmy Carr, Tom Daley and Natalie Imbruglia. Harry reportedly enjoyed flirting with Australian singer-songwriter Natalie. The two stars left the party together and apparently Harry received a cheer when he arrived at breakfast the following morning.

When quizzed about her night with Harry, Natalie said: 'Why are you asking me? Go ask him.'

Meanwhile, the next time Harry sang 'Torn' with the other 1D members, Grimmy was in the audience and he teased him, tweeting: 'They are doing a cover of Torn by Natalie Imbruglia. LOLLLLZZZZ.'

Harry later admitted to Alan Carr on his chat show that it might have looked a 'bit dodgy'. 'We were at a wedding, James Corden's wedding,' Harry told him. 'We'd never met before, and that was literally it. We had a drink. I guess we kinda left at the same time so it might have looked a bit dodgy.' He later told *Now* magazine that he fancied Natalie when he was younger. He said that while he has a lot of girls who are friends, they are not all girlfriends. However, he didn't dismiss his Lothario status, 'on the other hand, I'm eighteen and I'm having fun,' he admitted, 'I am young, after all.'

Being young also meant experimenting in other ways and he added to his ever-growing tattoo collection.

Zayn has always been a fan of body art and while the boys were in New Zealand earlier in the year he got a new tattoo on his neck, adding to his collection of five, including one in Arabic on his collarbone which means 'Be true to who you are' and his grandfather's name on his chest.

In July, Harry had an 'A' inked in the crook of his elbow, a tribute to his mum, along with the Temper Trap lyrics 'won't stop till we surrender' from the song 'Sweet Disposition' next to a star on his arm.

A month later, on the set of the video for 'Live While We're Young', he showed off a new one which appeared to be on his collarbone. Tattoo artist Kevin Paul, who also inks the likes of Ed Sheeran, JLS's Aston and Rizzle Kicks, told *Sugarscape* he was doing Harry a half sleeve.

'We're doing that now, so over the next week or two,' he explained. 'I'm gonna draw that up, send him the pictures over and then I'll go back down and start it up. There's nothing on his collarbone, it's at the top of the arm to begin the sleeve.'

He also said the collection had real meanings for Harry. Kevin explained: 'They're really personal to him – the reasons he had them done and stuff – so he doesn't really want to announce what they are. One was something from his childhood, and another one was something really important in his life. It's at the top of the arm to begin the sleeve. I tattooed Ed Sheeran as well – who did a little locket on Harry's hand, like a little padlock thing. They didn't really have to stop because of the pain, it was all pretty small things really so didn't take too long.' Showing his trust in his pal, Ed had actually inked Harry's arm at an earlier date at Kevin's parlour and the artist posted a picture on Instagram with the words: 'Then Ed tattooed Harry.'

In September, Harry showed off a picture of his left arm, where he had begun the sleeve of images. Among them was a black star, an iced gem, comedy and tragedy masks, a birdcage and the letters 'SMCL'. Some fans speculated that this means 'smile more, cry later' or is a reference to their boss, Simon Cowell. It wasn't known when he had them done, although he had paid a visit to the Shamrock Social Club tattoo parlour in West Hollywood, where he had his sister Gemma's name etched on his upper left arm in Hebrew by artist Isaiah Negrete.

He had visited the shop with *Glee* stars Kevin McHale and Jenna Ushkowitz and *Gossip Girl* actress Jessica Szohr, who appeared in a Twitter photo with the singer. Kevin tweeted: 'Tattoo crew! @jennaushkowitz @itsmejessicaszohr @harry_styles @lpthree.'

During an appearance on Irish chat show *The Late Late Show* in October, Harry revealed that he had been to a tattoo parlour earlier that day but refused to show the new tattoos off as they were still bandaged up. He also declined to say what they actually meant, but Niall said: 'It's a London thing.' He and his bandmates, with the exception of Niall, all have screw tattoos on their ankles.

Later in the year he got more tattoos at the Shamrock tattoo parlour, a favourite with David Beckham. He was dressed casually in jeans and a shirt but once he was inside he stripped down to his white vest, much to the delight of the fans outside. He was then seen looking through the different designs.

Afterwards he showed off two new inkings on his chest – two birds across his pecs. He told *US Weekly*: 'I did get some new tattoos! I got two swallows on my chest. I like that kind of style of tattoos, like the old sailor kind of tattoos. They symbolize travelling and we travel a lot.' He added that having an inking is very painful and 'anyone who says tattoos don't hurt is a liar!'

In October, 1D were back in LA for recording sessions and caused a stir when they were pictured just hours after they seemingly sang 'Little Things' on the UK *X Factor*, which was advertised as a live performance. The judges gave them a standing ovation and Dermot interviewed them while the audience screamed as if they were there. However, they had recorded it a few weeks previously and everything had been done to make it look completely authentic.

The boys did have advice for the 2012 wannabes and Harry made sure he told Union J's young singer George Shelley to leave his curly hair alone. Many comparisons were made between the two bands and *The Sun* said that Harry saw himself in George.

Union J's Josh Cuthbert said: 'We spoke to One Direction backstage. Liam was saying, "You guys are going to be so successful" and wished us all the best of luck. They're really nice lads. They're like friends; we're getting to know them. We've seen them a few times now. There's no rivalry there at all – we'd love to be as successful as them.'

Union J were probably hoping for a slice of 1D's success, especially when a few days later they were named as new entries in *Heat* magazine's list of '30 of the richest stars under 30'. In the number five spot after amassing a fortune of £26.3 million in the previous year, they were behind only huge acting stars Daniel Radcliffe, Robert Pattinson, Keira Knightley and Emma Watson.

Heat editor Lucie Cave said: 'In these financially tough times it's good to know that at least somebody is rolling around on carpets woven from gold-plated £50 notes. One Direction will be thrilled to hear they are the highest new entry. Like any pop stars they'll be after the number one spot, of course, but if they keep going the way they have been, that might be a reality in 2013.'

Proving just how close the boys are, and backing up the comments that they spend time together when they are not working, at the end of October Harry, Niall and Liam were seen supporting Louis as he played a charity football match in his hometown of Doncaster. Louis' team eventually won and the boys joined him for a victory lap around the stadium.

They then went on another short European tour, performing on *The X Factor Italy* in Milan, where they sang 'Live While We're Young' wearing coordinating colours in a palette of burgundy, blue, black and white. After the show, they attended a photocall at the Principe di Savoia hotel. On the way home Harry tweeted a picture of himself in the cockpit of the plane as a blonde girl kissed him on the cheek. Liam tweeted a picture of the band getting cosy under big duvets.

They then had their first interview and shoot with *Vogue* for a special edition of the glossy magazine, entitled 'Vogue Goes Pop'. This marked a serious transition for the group into an altogether more adult arena. The boys posed in sharp suits alongside model Edie Campbell, although a behind-the-scenes teaser showed them in more relaxed baseball attire.

Harry revealed that he enjoyed the fans screaming. He said: 'You're never going to get used to walking into a room and have people screaming at you. There's a lot of things that come with the life you could get lost in. But you have to let it be what it is. I've learnt not to take everything too seriously.'

He also commented on how he thinks his fashion sense has changed – and he is embarrassed about some of the things he wore when he first went on *The X Factor*. 'I like fashion. When I look back at the kind of stuff I wore on *The X Factor*, I laugh. There's no excuse.'

And while she was the envy of virtually every teenage girl around, Edie says she didn't fall for their charms and the group reminded her of her 'little sister's friends'.

Harry was the only one brave enough to talk to the model, who has worked for most of the major fashion houses and was famously shot alongside Kate Moss for Burberry by renowned fashion snapper Mario Testino.

She said: 'The others didn't really say much to me, just Harry. He looks so young, but he's so sweet. The hair was very prominent – it was swept back like lots of teenage boys wear it. The hair was impressive. He left me hanging at the end of the day though. We went to say goodbye and I gave him a kiss on the cheek, I went into the right and then to the left – like you do in fashion, the double kiss – and by the time I'd got round to the left, he'd disappeared. There was no serenade; no What Makes You Beautiful, nothing.'

Sadly she was forced to delete her Twitter account afterwards when jealous fans sent her messages, including one who said she looked 'like a 40-year-old troll'. However, the model took it in her stride and explained: 'As long as they don't appear at my door with fire-lit torches, I reckon I can handle it.'

The boys also starred in *Teen Vogue* and they all got their own covers. Harry was wearing a tweed jacket and striped shirt for his. He revealed the length some fans go to in order to spend time with him.

He told them: 'One time, a girl dropped her phone in my pocket, and I found it and was like, "There you go." And she said, "If you'd had my phone, you'd have had to meet up with me to give it back." It's nice to have people go to these lengths for you, but sometimes it's hard to understand, because we're just guys. We're guys who would be at your school, who got this amazing opportunity.'

The boys loved the laid-back vibe of being in the studio, getting their make-up and hair done and posing in front of the cameras. It was a far cry from jumping around on stage but often came as a welcome break.

Clearly the other women's magazines were also honing in on the boys' selling power and not long after *Vogue* they became the first stars to grace an all-male *Cosmopolitan* magazine cover, for which Harry took the central spot in a maroon t-shirt, white cardi and smart navy blazer, sandwiched between Zayn and Liam on his left and Louis and Niall on his right. The lads had picked up an award for Ultimate Men of the Year at the *Cosmo* Ultimate Women of the Year Awards and Harry admitted that being called a ladies' man doesn't annoy him.

'I feel so lucky to be in this position,' he explained. 'I'm not entitled to be annoyed. I'm not half as busy as they make me out to be! A lot of time the way it's portrayed is that I only see women in a sexual way. But I grew up with just my mum and sister so I respect women a lot.'

The magazine's editor, Louise Court, said she was very surprised because unlike other cover stars, who are often late and demanding, the boys offered to make her a cup of tea and were half an hour early for their shoot!

The start of November marked the release of their second album, *Take Me Home*, which had already landed the No. 1 spot on the pre-order charts in fifty countries.

It opens with 'Live While We're Young', track two is the upbeat and cheeky 'Kiss You' and acoustic 'Little Things' written by Ed Sheeran is the third offering. The fourth track is 'C'mon C'mon', the most dancey single on the album with a thumping bass, and Harry's vocals really stand out. 'Last First Kiss' – which has a rousing interlude from Harry and was co-written by Louis, Liam and Zayn – is followed by 'Heart Attack', co-produced by the man behind Taylor Swift's recent single, 'We Are Never Ever Getting Back Together'. Number eight is the moody 'Change My Mind' and track nine is 'I Would', a pop-rock song, with some whistling bits, penned by McFly's Tom Fletcher, Dougie Poynter and Danny Jones. Number ten is 'Over Again', the second Ed Sheeran song and again, it is toned down and more melodic and you can really hear the vocals. Tracks eleven and twelve are 'Back for You', co-written by the boys, and classic boyband ballad 'They Don't Know About Us', and the final song is 'Summer Love', a slow pop number with an upbeat anthemic chorus. Harry's favourite tracks on the album are 'Little Things' and 'Heart Attack'.

It was reviewed well by the critics, who were divided over how much the boys' music had evolved since their first album. The BBC called it 'polished and dependable, despite its safety there are some show-stopping pop anthems present, with the instantaneous chorus of "C'Mon C'Mon" perhaps the best thing 1D have put their name to.'

The Washington Post said: 'It's a contagious singalong, with no one voice leading the charge, no frontman, no star. They harmonize like the world's first socialist boyband. Something else that sets One Direction apart from 'N Sync, the Backstreet Boys and generations of chart-topping heart-throbs before them: They appear immune to outside contemporary influences.'

The Huffington Post added: 'The album feels relentless in rhythm, sometimes even during the ballads, with a homogeneous sound and message – like a teenage boy who says all the right words in a rush to get what he wants. But this time they're only singing the right words to get to your wallets and adoration. And they're most likely going to get it.'

However, if they ever needed any reassurance that the critics' reviews aren't everything, here it was: the album topped the charts in thirty-five countries and sold over a million copies in its first week worldwide. In the UK it sold 155,000 copies in the first week and became the group's first album to land the No. 1 spot in the charts, and in the US it debuted in the top spot on the *Billboard* 200 chart, with the third-largest debut sales ever in one week, behind Taylor Swift's *Red* and Mumford & Sons' *Babel*. It marked the first time that a UK group had ever achieved a No. 1 record on release in the 54-year history of the chart.

Furthermore, One Direction was the second act of 2012 to notch a pair of No. 1 albums within twelve months: Justin Bieber's *Believe* and *Under the Mistletoe* both topped the chart within eight months of each other. The number of albums the band was shifting seemed almost inconceivable to Harry and the others.

Hilariously, Harry had tried to buy the album – at the modest price of £7.99 – to boost sales during the week of release but his card was rejected. He took to his Twitter page to share the news and wrote: 'Soooo . . . I went to download our album this morning. And my card got declined. Hahaha!!'

However, as soon as he found out they had landed the top spot he was quick to thank the fans, writing: 'Hello . . . Thank you so much for all your support with this album. We can't believe the number ones today! Thank you thank you. Huge Love. xx'.

People everywhere were talking about the boys' groundbreaking success and Mick Jagger – who Harry is often compared to – commented to CNN that the boys reminded him of the legendary Rolling Stones.

'I watched a concert of One Direction on TV the other night, you know, just to check [it] out,' he said. 'It reminded me very much of our early concerts, when we were pushed around among the audience and we would kind of float. They were like floating above the audience, and they looked really distinctly uncomfortable.'

He added: 'I remember feeling that same uncomfortable feeling of being pushed around in this very weird place about fifty years ago. It was a very funny moment, because it was very similar to the things we've been through.'

'Little Things' was their second single from the album to be released, on 11 November, and it got its first airplay on Grimmy's show on Radio 1. A slower and more stripped-back song, it talks about loving a girl's insecurities.

Ed Sheeran wrote it with another singer and songwriter called Fiona Bevan when he was seventeen. He said the song 'is about the best things about someone, kind of like things you wouldn't expect'. He also commented that the boys wanted to 'switch it up a bit'. And he loves the lyrics that Harry sings, one of his favourite lines written in a song begins: 'I know you never like the sound of your voice on tape and you never like to know how much you weigh . . .'

The video was shot in black and white and directed by Vaughan Arnell again. It shows the boys in a recording studio; Harry is wearing a checked shirt and sits at the mixing desk, altering the sound.

Although the single was met with mixed reviews, it became the boys' second UK No. 1 – and the album and the single debuted simultaneously at No. 1 in the UK. One Direction became the youngest act in British chart history to achieve this spectacular feat.

The boys performed a heartfelt live rendition of the single at the Royal Albert Hall for the hundredth Royal Variety Performance, sitting on lit-up stools.

David Walliams was hosting the event and dressed up as a crazy female stalker, much to the hilarity of the audience. Putting on his best lady's voice, he said: 'I've got a washing machine and I named it One Direction. You make me so happy. Was your song 'What Makes You Beautiful' written about me? I love you so much. Will you marry me?'

Looking smart in black suits, 1D were lucky enough to meet the Queen afterwards, alongside some of the other acts who had performed, including Robbie Williams and Girls Aloud. Harry admitted: 'I s*** myself', while Cheryl said the monarch had 'hair like candyfloss and tiny little dancing-style shoes'.

Harry posted a picture of himself alongside small comedian Ronnie Corbett, with the caption 'what a legend'. Later Harry took to Twitter again and wrote: 'Amazing night. Can't believe it. Night! .xx.'

They also performed on BBC's *Children in Need*, where they opened the show with a rendition of 'Live While We're Young' and later sang 'Little Things'.

Harry's mane of hair was always the subject of much discussion and he had said he would get rid of it for charity, although his management team argued strongly against it.

'I want to shave my hair off and no-one will really let me. Everyone's telling me not to do it. My argument is like, I think my popularity is in my face, and not my hair.' After these revelations fans flocked to Twitter to beg him to reconsider.

One wrote: 'Noo Harry, don't shave your hair off before I touch it :) pleaseeeee@Harry_Styles', and another fan added: 'and you should never cut your hair because I like the way you flick it off@Harry_Styles.'

Children in Need presenter Fearne Cotton took the opportunity to tease him about it, saying: 'So I've heard that you, Harry, will shave your head for Children in Need!' and after looking awkward for a few seconds, he replied: 'Sure, go for it if you want.' Luckily for him, she was only joking and put the clippers down, saying: 'I can't! I can't be responsible for that! Can you imagine?'

The evening was a huge success. Thanks to the boys and other guests and the generous public, they raised a huge £26.7 million for the Children in Need charity.

The boys announced their 2013 Take Me Home tour, which sees them play 116 dates in 19 countries. Kicking off at The O2 arena, it includes a whopping 38 dates in the UK, after the huge demand meant they had to add extra shows, and 39 in America and Canada. Tickets sales reached 300,000

within a day of release, including sold-out dates at the huge
O2 arena, and tickets for the shows in Perth in Australia sold
out in six minutes.

The boys are only set to get four or five days off each
month during the tour and critics started to talk about them
getting burnt out. Andy Greene of *Rolling Stone* said: 'I've
never known a band to announce a second summer tour
before the first tour is over. It's insane – they're working
them like dogs and printing money right now.'

LA-based media commentator Mike Raia added: 'One
Direction are being touted here as The Beatles of their gen-
eration. That's one mighty heavy load to bear. There is a
definite risk of burnout unless they are allowed some time
off to let off steam. It would be heart-rending to see them
fall apart.'

Fans also voiced their concern. But the boys have
always maintained that they feel so lucky to have the opportunity and are prepared to work as hard as they need to.
Simon has always insisted that their management will be
sensible and treat them well because, unlike in previous
years when boybands only lasted two or three years, he sees
a long future ahead of them.

They may have been working hard but they were also
having as much fun as ever and managed to get #Piers
MorganIsSmelly trending worldwide on Twitter after they
clashed over the footballer David Beckham.

Piers originally sent a message to his followers saying
that David should give up. He wrote: 'No serious top-

flight team would sign Beckham for football reasons any more – he should retire gracefully.'

Harry saw it and replied: 'Beckham is my hero. Winston is second in line.'

Piers responded: 'Is that because he always runs in one direction?'

Louis then waded in, adding: 'I LOVE David Beckham!'

Piers quipped back: 'Well sign him up for the group – bet he sings better than he plays now,' before adding: 'Can't believe I'm currently being sledged about Beckham by TWO members of One Direction. Boy-band types clearly stick together.'

Harry then wrote to Simon, penning: "Hiiii @SimonCowell can you tell @piersmorgan to leave us alone please? He's being nasty.'

Niall also joined in writing: 'Do u just live on twitter! What else do you do in the day?', to which Piers replied: 'I listen to music by The Wanted.'

Piers then found himself subject to the anger of the loyal Directioners.

'Now got roughly 25 million One Directioners abusing me – many thanks @Harry_Styles @Real_Liam_Payne @Louis_Tomlinson.'

However, he was quick to challenge the boys to come on his show and settle the argument when Liam urged fans on to get #PiersMorganIsSmelly trending worldwide. Piers said: 'So, #PiersMorganIsSmelly is now trending worldwide, is it? Right, @Harry_Styles @Real_Liam_

Payne @Louis_Tomlinson – this is WAR. Let's settle this on my CNN show when you come to New York – if you're brave enough.'

But Liam responded, saying: 'No hard feelings stinky.'

CHAPTER ELEVEN

'I just bumped into Taylor in a zoo and then I don't know . . .'

All-American girl Taylor Swift was born on 13 December 1989 in Pennsylvania. She was desperate to be a singer and from the age of eleven she tried to make a career in music, posting demo tapes to every record producer in America's country-music capital, Nashville. Even though they rejected her, she forged ahead, determined to make it.

After her family moved to Nashville when she was four-teen, she was spotted singing at the country's famous Bluebird Cafe and became the youngest songwriter ever to be hired by Sony. A record deal followed shortly after. She released her eponymous debut album in 2006, cementing her status as a star.

By the time she met Harry in March 2012, she was one of the US's biggest female singers, having sold more than 23 million albums. She has been described as 'America's sweetheart' and 'a role model' and is worth a staggering $100 million. In 2009 she broke Beyoncé's record for the most top-forty singles by a single artist and has netted six Grammys.

Her most recent album, *Red*, achieved the highest opening sales in a decade – making her the first female singer to have two million-selling albums. It also became her first UK No. 1 album.

Taylor has had a number of high-profile relationships, which have inspired some of her music and lyrics. She has previously dated Joe Jonas, Taylor Lautner, John Mayer and Jake Gyllenhaal. After splitting with John she wrote the single 'Dear John', and after her much-publicised split with Joe, who apparently dumped her over the phone, she posted a Myspace video with a *Camp Rock* doll based on the character he played in the 2008 Disney movie of the same name. In the video she holds up the plastic model and says: 'See, this one even comes with a phone, so he can break up with other dolls.'

After a string of failed romances, Taylor now knows what she wants from a relationship. She told *Harper's Bazaar*: 'I like a man to take control. It needs to be equal. If I feel too much like I'm wearing the pants, I start to feel uncomfortable and we break up.'

Taylor has also spoken of her desire to settle down. She told *Cosmopolitan* magazine: 'I think that the idea of finding another person to share your life with is the most fascinating, beautiful quest you could ever be on in life. And yes, living your dreams is so important too, and a lot of times I've put that before everything else.

'But then you get to a place where the whole time you're living these dreams, you look beside you to say to someone, "Hey, isn't this so much fun?!" And if there's no one there to say it to, what's the point? Being a mom full time, doing everything for my kids, having a bunch of them. One day, I'm sure. But that's the only other thing that could be as thrilling for me as doing this.'

She is also good friends with the boys' pal Ed Sheeran, after they collaborated on her album *Red* together.

She told the *Daily Mail*'s *You* magazine: 'Ed Sheeran and I wrote a duet called "Everything Has Changed" while sitting on a trampoline in my back yard. It's a lot easier than you think.

'We had one guitar, which we passed back and forth, and then we baked an apple pie, or rather my friends and I baked it and Ed watched and then ate it afterwards. His performance at the Olympic closing ceremony was incredible – I really think that was his big breakthrough moment in the US.'

Taylor also posted pictures of her and Ed together on Twitter and he will guest on her 45-date Red world tour in 2013.

After Harry and Taylor first met he coyly described her as 'nice', and she had been seen dancing along to 1D's performance at the Nickelodeon Kids' Choice Awards and at the Radio 1 Teen Awards earlier in the year.

At the Nickelodeon Awards, apparently she told Justin Bieber how much she fancied Harry, while Justin joked about keeping his girlfriend – Selena Gomez – away from the band. Apparently Taylor went backstage and said hi to the guys in their dressing room, and made everyone laugh by dramatically fanning herself afterwards.

Justin said: 'I already know one of the biggest artists in the world thinks Harry is so hot but I have been sworn to secrecy.'

Harry had always voiced the fact that he found Taylor attractive, and after they met he told *Seventeen* magazine: 'She honestly couldn't be a sweeter person. She's genuinely nice and extremely talented, and she deserves everything she has.'

Later, it emerged that the couple may have had a fling after this, while Harry was in the States, so she was heart-broken when she saw pictures of Harry kissing Emma Ostilly in New Zealand, but she later hooked up with Conor Kennedy – JFK's great-nephew.

A source told *Radar Online*: 'Taylor really liked Harry and even though they weren't exclusive, he hinted at making it official with her just before he took off to Australia. He even told Taylor he didn't want her to see anybody else while he was gone.'

After rumours they had been texting one another, he was asked about it on an Australian radio show, and he said at the time: 'We met in America, and she's very nice . . .' Later it was noted that they wore the same necklace just days after each other.

Then, early in November, they were seen holding hands backstage on the US *X Factor*, where they were both due to perform. During rehearsals, Harry even joined Taylor's entourage and mum Andrea in the audience to watch her soundcheck before running on stage, tackling her, throwing her over his shoulder and dashing off with her.

Radio-show host Mario Lopez confirmed he saw the pair 'walking hand in hand', telling listeners: 'Taylor Swift was the special guest performer, and [here's] a little inside scoop for you. During rehearsals, Harry from One Direction came and slapped me on the back, and said, "Hey, Mario, how ya doing?" And I said, "What are you doing here?" And he sort of [pointed] toward Taylor.'

Mario said he later saw them 'walking off hand in hand. So Taylor Swift and Harry from One Direction – you heard it here first. [They're] officially hanging out, I can say that much.'

And the official US *X Factor* Twitter page sent Twitter-sphere into meltdown with the words: 'Together in the lunch line (Cheeseburgers) laughing & smiling was @Harry_Styles & @taylorswift13! :) #internationalpoproyalty'.

The pair were quickly dubbed Haylor and officially knocked Justin Bieber and Selena Gomez off the pedestal of coolest celeb couple. The inevitable tweets flooded in, some even threatening to 'kill' Taylor. One wrote: 'if u dating my Harry, I kill you,' while another said: 'I'll murder Taylor Swift. She will not date my Harry.'

The boys' performance of 'Live While We're Young' amid red London telephone boxes and balloons made host Khloe Kardashian swoon and ask: 'How hot are One Direction?'

More speculation ensued, with *Look* magazine claiming that Taylor had instructed an estate agent to find her a home near Harry's pad in north London, but then the couple were snapped publicly together for the first time in early December, enjoying a romantic stroll through New York's iconic Central Park whilst visiting the zoo, hugging a friend's baby. They looked totally loved up. Harry was wearing his trademark beanie, a shirt and a khaki jacket and Taylor was dressed down in a burgundy jacket.

The boys had arrived in New York at the end of November and went through the airport surrounded by thickset body-guards. Harry led the group, in navy jeans and a brown shirt that revealed the wing-tips of his bird tattoos. He looked like he'd just woken up from a nap, wearing two jackets and with the hood of his blue sweatshirt covering most of his famous tousled brown locks.

Truly cementing their iconic status was the pop-up shop, called 1D World, that opened next to the Madison Square Garden arena, stocking nothing but One Direction merchandise, including promo t-shirts, hoodies and even onesies. For $30, fans could walk away with a life-size cut-out of Harry.

Fans took their loyalty to a new level when many camped

outside the Rockefeller Plaza five days ahead of the band's appearance on the *Today* show. Again, armed with sleeping bags, tents, banners and food supplies, they started to block traffic lanes and cause the inevitable chaos. They were given wristbands with numbers and told to go away and come back at 2 a.m. to get a spot in the show's production area.

The power of social media was all too evident as endless pictures of the boys were posted on Instagram. Presenter Al Roker said: 'We have never, ever had a crowd this big. This one breaks all records.'

They performed a three-song set, including 'What Makes You Beautiful', 'Live While We're Young' and fan favourite 'Little Things'. Harry thanked the fans for their unending support and paid tribute to everyone who had been affected by Hurricane Sandy, which swept across the Caribbean and destroyed whole communities in coastal New York and New Jersey.

'I think in spite of everything that's happened, our thoughts and prayers are with everyone that's been affected by Hurricane Sandy and to see everyone come out still when everything's happened is absolutely amazing,' he said. 'It means so much to us.'

Monday 3 December was another date to go down in One Direction history as 20,000 fans congregated from all corners of the globe at New York's Madison Square Garden to see them sing. Previous performers at the historic venue include The Beatles, Kanye West and the Rolling Stones. The concert was also webcast live on Ustream.

Entertainment Weekly wrote: 'The real noise in the arena came from the thousands of screaming girls there to empty their lungs at each and every opportunity. (At one point a teen behind me screamed her brains out and then shrieked, "I don't even know why I'm screaming!!!" I didn't know either. One Direction was not scheduled to take the stage for another hour.)'

The US critics loved it. The *New York Daily News* noted the lack of production but said it just added to the relaxed approach: 'The screams were louder than a jet engine, with a pitch higher than a banshee's wail. Despite the event's significance, a certain casualness informed the staging. Unlike boybands of the past, these guys aren't rigidly choreographed in concert, an appealing aspect. They jump and stroll rather than dance.'

The large tour bus picked up Taylor and the other girlfriends – Danielle, Eleanor and Perrie – and the boys' families, and they all travelled together to the after-party at New York's Hudson hotel. Harry's dad, Des, had flown out to watch the gig and spent a few days with the boys in the 1D van. Taylor had come straight from an annual gala event – hosted by her ex Conor Kennedy's famous family – where she was awarded the 2012 Ripple of Hope Award. She was wearing a little black dress and looked every inch the perfect pop star girlfriend.

The girls, friends and family went through the main entrance for the swanky celebratory bash, while the boys and Taylor sneaked through the back door. Harry then

introduced his new superstar love to his mum Anne, and
the smitten duo were said to have recreated the Dirty
Dancing lift to the song '(I've Had) The Time of My Life'
on the dance floor while other guests laughed and egged
them on. Harry was also seen singing a very bad version of
Elton John and Kiki Dee's 'Don't Go Breaking My Heart'
on the karaoke machine with Ed Sheeran (who sang all the
high bits!) while Taylor looked on.

After the lavish party, the couple were spotted holding
hands returning to Taylor's hotel at 4 a.m. and the following
day they emerged though the lobby doors just moments
apart. That night, Harry was seen arriving at Taylor's hotel
with his head down and an overnight bag slung over his
shoulder at 11 p.m., just an hour after she had finished doing
some recording at New York's Pier 59 Studios. The following morning he emerged in a fresh white 'London Loves LA'
t-shirt and a slightly messy hairdo, surrounded by his minders.

Later he snubbed female fans outside the Ed Sullivan
Theater, where they had gathered to see Harry and the boys
after their appearance on *The Late Show with David Letterman*.
While Zayn and Liam were seen posing for photos, Harry
walked straight past, as did Niall and Louis, hurrying to the
waiting car. As much as Harry loved talking to his fans, some
days he was just tired and not up to it.

During their interview on David Letterman's show, the
boys shared the sofa with legendary Hollywood actor Dustin
Hoffman, who hilariously went in for a playful snog with

Niall, as the other boys fell around laughing. After a straight-forward chat introducing them and talking about their experiences they sang 'Little Things' to the studio audience.

That night Harry and Taylor were spotted again, leaving Taylor's hotel on their way to a romantic dinner date. Harry was dressed in a black fur-collared jacket, brown t-shirt and blue jeans, while his girlfriend wore a brown jacket over a dress and stripey tights. From dinner they went to the Crosby Street Hotel, where they were met by some of Taylor's friends including actresses Emma Stone and Dianna Agron.

Taylor had previously spoken about her friendship with Emma, saying to *Harper's Bazaar*: 'We never talk about fash-ion, about career, about ambition or our projects. We just talk about relationships, feelings, love and boys.'

She has also said in the past: 'I am totally a girl's girl. My girlfriends have stopped me making a lot of bad choices. Your girlfriends are objective, they don't feel the desperate passionate feelings you're feeling.'

So no doubt the girls knew exactly how Taylor was feel-ing about Harry – but clearly they also approved of her new man.

As the world buzzed with the news of the couple, Ed Sheeran answered the question on everyone's lips when he was asked about them, nodding before saying: 'I mean, the papers are saying it.'

1D had one final appearance in New York on 7 December at Z100's Jingle Ball at Madison Square Garden, where they treated fans to their four biggest hits – 'Live While We're Young', 'One Thing', 'Little Things' and 'What Makes You Beautiful'. They were followed by performances from Olly Murs, Cher Lloyd and Taylor, who invited Ed on to the stage for the song they wrote together. Justin Bieber closed the show.

On the red carpet Harry joked about with a sprig of mistletoe, kissing girls who walked past. When he was asked what he thought about the amount of attention the relationship was getting, he coyly responded: 'I just bumped into her at the zoo and then I don't know . . .' There are pictures of Taylor backstage, giving Harry a kiss on the cheek before he bounded on stage with the rest of 1D.

Later Harry managed to tear himself away from Taylor, and the boys were seen larking around Central Park making a home video of themselves. At one point Harry hugged a Statue of Liberty impersonator, and he was also seen being lifted by his minders while styling his famous curls.

From there the boys headed back to the UK for the Capital FM Jingle Bell Ball and, rather than travelling with the others on a domestic flight, Harry accepted a ride on Taylor's private jet which whisked the couple from New York to London. Liam, Niall, Louis and Zayn touched down at Heathrow before getting into a waiting car. Unusually, instead of speaking to fans they dashed past and there was a huge scrum.

Liam tweeted a photo of his arm, which was scratched by a fan. He wrote: 'I don't know why people are blaming us for this it's so sad :(when everyone's rushing and make it unsafe we get thrown back in our cars. That was actually horrible I literally wanted to cry and all those people shouting s**t at us and we even tried to stop so s**t. Girls with the sign tho very nice welcome :) thank you No more sad tweets now tho lets all be calm next time then we can meet you guys. Good news is we will probably see you all later anyway :) so smiles all round and nobody got hurt.'

They had just a few hours to rehearse for the Jingle Bell Ball and they performed dressed casually in jeans and t-shirts. They kicked their set off with 'C'mon C'mon' and Harry shouted to the crowd: 'London make some noise! It feels great to be back in the UK! You guys are absolutely amazing. Thank you for having us. Let's have a bit of fun shall we?' They then went on to sing 'Live While We're Young' and performed a funny *Inbetweeners* dance routine during the song's middle section. They launched into 'Kiss You' while confetti fell from the ceiling, followed by 'What Makes You Beautiful' and wrapped up with 'Little Things'.

Taylor was whisked to the VIP area to watch the event, which featured performances by JLS, Little Mix, Rizzle Kicks and Cheryl Cole, who duetted with her manager, will.i.am. Later the boys from the band Lawson posted a snap of themselves with her.

The Wanted were also there, and when asked about their feud, Max said: 'We try not to react too much to petty banter like that.' However, Jay was slightly more conciliatory and said that in the spirit of the festive season, it was time to put their differences behind them.

He told MTV News: 'It seemed to start as a joke. But then the tone got a little bit nasty, so I just like to see how they feel about it, because I didn't like what I read. I think it's probably best that we peace a little at Christmas. Peace and love at Christmas!'

Rumours surfaced that while Harry was happy to spend hours canoodling with his new love, the rest of the band were less than impressed with the time they were spending together. Taylor was later branded as the band's Yoko Ono, comparing her with John Lennon's artist wife who was said to be responsible for The Beatles' split in 1970.

But the boys are always quick to say they would never split up or leave the group, maintaining that they are dedicated to 1D and their fans – although they had made reference to taking a break in the future and getting back together ten years later, emulating Take That.

Despite being compared to Robbie Williams, Harry insists he doesn't see himself like the singer. 'I don't look at myself as the Robbie Williams of the band. I don't think that kind of comparison is on any of our minds. I just can't think about life beyond One Direction at the moment. It's going so well and we are like brothers.'

However, Robbie says he feels sorry for Harry because of the attention he gets. Speaking to *The Sun*, he said: 'I feel a bit for Harry. At his age I was in this lilywhite boyband, Take That. But I was meeting up with mates, jumping out

of the tour bus and into a Transit van at the motorway service stations all around the country … It's not a secret any more
but I would get off my face and have complete anonymity. No
one had a camera phone so I could enjoy myself properly.
Harry is finding out it's not so easy for him.'

It was rumoured that the boys have signed a legally
binding document, which means that if any of them leave
within three years, they will all suffer financially. A source
told *The Sun*: 'It's a really clever contract that the boys
have signed up to. It means they have a real incentive to
tough it out and stick together. The formal length is for 36
months and an album a year – but the clever part is they
get the big payday after the three years. If one of them
walks away before then, then all five miss out on the
money. They don't miss out on a few quid either; we are
talking millions. They all get on really well, but it would
be the kind of deal that would see them through the worst
aggro possible.'

The next time Harry was seen with Taylor was backstage
at the *X Factor* final in Manchester on 9 December. 1D sang
'Kiss You' in matching black-and-white outfits to an audience
of 10,000 at the packed Manchester Central arena. The con-
test saw Jahmene Douglas battle James Arthur for the reality
crown, and James eventually triumphed.

1D's performance wasn't without its technical errors and
Zayn's microphone cut out, while Harry was said to have hit
the most bum notes – eight – during the performance,
according to AQA 63336, the UK's most accurate question

and answer service. Apparently Liam hit seven duff notes, Zayn hit five, Niall two and Louis one.

Harry may have hit a few flat notes, but Brian Friedman confirmed what all his fans know – Harry is the best dancer of the group. He told *The Sun*: 'Harry was definitely the best dancer. He was always good at the choreography. Niall was good at remembering which direction to move in.'

Next up was a magical mini-break for the couple, who headed north so Harry could introduce Taylor to his sister, Gemma. Harry and Gemma are extremely close and he really wanted her to meet his new girlfriend. While he is away he always texts Gemma and they share a love of music.

Harry told *Billboard*: 'I actually get a lot of music from my sister who's into all these bands. A lot of times suggested stuff comes on iTunes I'll have a look at it, or the fans will send me things. But I've been listening to The Lumineers. I love their album and also Elvis Perkins, he's great.'

While they were away the pair got to spend Taylor's twenty-third birthday together. Stepping out for a celebratory lunch, Harry looked thrilled as he took her for a meal at the George & Dragon in Great Budworth, Cheshire. Taylor looked gorgeous in a pea green coat, skinny jeans and stylish brogues as she held hands with Harry. She was overheard telling Gemma, 'He's amazing.'

Harry was said to have bought her gifts worth £1,000, including a £400 Jimmy Choo handbag, antique earrings and a vintage photo frame containing a black-and-white photo of them. He apparently also surprised her with twenty-three cupcakes which he'd personally picked out from a bakery.

The Custom Cupcake Company owner Matt Blakeley said: 'The woman [who ordered the cupcakes] said it was for Harry Styles but I didn't know who that was at first. We had got a lot of orders before Christmas, but she said she desperately needed them so we said OK.'

The birthday came at the end of their trip, which saw Harry show Taylor around the local area. Dressed up for the cold weather, they enjoyed a day in picturesque Bowness-on-Windermere where they strolled through the village, stopping at the Pandora jewellery shop and the World of Beatrix Potter, and they were pictured feeding doves together with Harry's mum. One of the birds took a peck at Taylor's new handbag, also thought to be a present from Harry.

The following day they went for a walk in the Peak District and had dinner with Gemma at The Rising Sun in Hope Valley where Taylor apparently tucked into the local delicacy – black pudding – followed by lemon sole, while Harry devoured a turkey roast followed by Christmas pudding.

Pub manager Sarah Walker explained: 'Taylor said she was loving being in Britain and she also seemed to like being in the countryside. She said she didn't mind the cold. They were both lovely and she's a honey.'

While she was in the UK, Harry was said to have got

Taylor hooked on one of his favourite comedy TV pro-
grammes, *The Inbetweeners*, which she found really funny.

Harry later drove Taylor to Manchester Airport, where
her private jet was waiting to take her to Germany for work
commitments. He went on to a university party thrown by
one of his friends in Sheffield. He arrived at 1.30 a.m. – and
immediately became the centre of attention as girls queued
to have their picture taken with him. He even showed off his
domestic side and did some washing-up. However, despite
the attention from other girls, Grimmy confirmed that he
was smitten with Taylor, telling the *Mirror*: 'Harry really
likes Taylor, he's fallen for her in a big way. At first I wasn't
sure if the relationship was a real one but I talk to him a lot
and it seems to be that she's the one for him – for now,
anyway.'

He also praised her fun attitude, adding: 'American artists
are usually really, really boring and reserved but Taylor is
fun. She's always up for a laugh and is really good company.

'Harry likes people who make him laugh. I talk to Harry
a lot on the phone while he's away touring and he talks
about her a lot. He is very happy with her. I like her a lot too,
she came on my show recently and we had a really fun
time.'

A day later it was back to work as the boys reunited to do
some filming in London on the banks of the River Thames,
before they jetted back to LA, where Harry was pictured leaving LAX airport in an orange beanie, a Rush t-shirt and jeans.
He returned to the Shamrock tattoo parlour with Taylor in

tow and had a large ship etched on his upper arm, next to the heart on his bicep. The design is really similar to the one the male model had on his arm in Taylor's video for the single 'I Knew You Were Trouble'. Harry posed for a series of snaps with the parlour owner and Taylor, who had been playing pool with friends while her man got the artwork done.

Next up was a performance at the final of the US *X Factor*. As they walked the red carpet Harry was asked how Taylor was and he replied: 'She's good,' while his bandmates mocked him, saying: 'Oh yes, so what do you think of the Haylor situation then?' Another interviewer asked if they were a couple and in a typical laid-back way, he confirmed they were.

In the studio, they performed 'Kiss Me' on a giant pair of bright red lips. Later Harry consoled one of the losing groups, girlband Fifth Harmony, by tweeting them: 'You were amazing. You're going to be great. Have a great night xxx'. He also congratulated the eventual winner, Tate Stevens.

He then went to stay with Taylor's family. Harry, Taylor and her mum Andrea were seen going grocery shopping, and later in the day Harry went through the drive-thru of popular fast-food chain In-N-Out Burger.

Showing just how quickly things were moving between them, the couple jetted off for a romantic skiing holiday in Utah, where they were seen having lunch with Taylor's brother Austin at the Canyons Resort in Park City. Harry stood out from the crowd in his orange beanie, while Taylor kept her head warm with a fashionable grey headband. Fans kept each other updated on what was happening between the pair on Twitter. One onlooker said: 'Harry was holding hands with tswift. I saw him first in hot tub outside my condo then on the streets downtown.'

While they were there the couple met up with Justin Bieber and Selena Gomez, who were staying in the same resort, The Colony.

It was rumoured that Harry and Taylor planned to spend Christmas together in Australia, as Taylor was going there to promote her new album and play some gigs. However, after a couple of days on the slopes Harry came home to spend Christmas with his family. He did his best not to attract attention to himself at the airport and appeared to have his chin tucked in a high-neck black sweater. On Christmas Eve he showed off a bandage on the same part of his face, only posting a cryptic message of 'Chin chinnigan, chin chinnigan . . .', making some people question if he'd fallen over while on the slopes.

Although Harry wasn't with Taylor at Christmas, he reportedly sent her a singagram to let her know he was thinking of her – and she found it hilarious. They were also said to have had a long Skype session on their computers.

Taylor was reported to have bought Harry some Beatles memorabilia after looking for rare autographed items she knew that he would love from shops in Liverpool. She was apparently looking to spend between £40,000 and £50,000. Harry also went vintage and bought Taylor an antique emerald bracelet he found in a jewellery store in Cheshire.

He may have more money than most teenagers can dream of but Harry likes to keep his wishes simple – he asked for pants for Christmas! He told MTV: 'I just asked for pants and socks, because if you're on the road you always run out of pants and socks.'

On Boxing Day, Harry went with his dad, Olly Murs and some guys from his management team to watch Manchester United play at Old Trafford. Two days later and he was set to jet back out to the US to see in the New Year with Taylor, who was performing alongside Justin Bieber for *Dick Clark's New Year's Rockin' Eve* in Times Square, New York.

His mum drove him to Heathrow Airport but it seems he might have been in too much of a rush, as he left his passport at home! Even though he got a courier to go and pick it up rather than drive back up north with Anne, he ended up being forced to wait until 7.30 p.m., when the next available flight left, rather than taking the 11.15 a.m. flight to Boston as he had planned. He was seen walking through the airport in his beanie and a black jacket and was understandably annoyed with himself; some days he felt that all he did was travel and wait in airports.

When he arrived Harry nipped into Jay-Z and Coldplay's New Year's Eve concert in Brooklyn, along with Cheryl Cole and Christina Aguilera, but rushed back across the river to Manhattan to see Taylor perform. She had ditched her preppy look for tight black leather trousers and a red jacket and sang her heart out. After Taylor's performance the couple shared a passionate kiss. One fan tweeted: 'Just rode on an elevator with Harry Styles and Taylor Swift while they made out. It was beautiful.'

The loved-up pair got amongst the crowds in Times Square to see the New Year crystal ball drop and shared another snog before heading to back their hotel, where Harry apparently declared his love for his new girlfriend. He was really falling for her and knew that she understood exactly what he was going through. Taylor was also clearly thrilled at how her year was going and tweeted: 'Can't even verbalize how stoked I am for 2013!'

However Taylor's protective father Scott reportedly ordered Harry to slow things down during a man-to-man chat because he didn't want his daughter's heart to be broken.

A 'source' told *The Sun on Sunday*: 'He likes Harry but he wants them to slow down and take things easy. It's clear to everyone they are smitten with one another and are already talking about marriage. He doesn't want them to split up.'

The New Year started with another jaunt in the sun when Harry and Taylor jetted off to the British Virgin Islands on New Year's Day for a top-secret holiday. They had both been so busy they needed some time away to relax and they hoped that no one would know where they went.

It was only revealed that the pair were there when pictures emerged on the Internet of them posing with some fans at a restaurant in Virgin Gorda, the third largest of the Caribbean islands. In the snaps Taylor is wearing a mint green spaghetti strap dress and her signature red lippy and Harry is sporting his favourite orange beanie hat.

While he was away, Harry was also pictured on the beach topless showing even more tattoos, including the inkings 'might as well' on his torso, 'LA, NY and LDN' – references to cities he has performed in – on his shoulder and 'Can I cry?'

However, pictures then emerged of a downcast and upset-looking Taylor alone on a boat at Virgin Gorda's US Customs with her hands in her lap, while Harry partied in a hot tub on Necker Island with friends and family of the island's billionaire owner, Richard Branson.

Some claimed the couple were on the rocks after Taylor cryptically tweeted some lyrics from her single 'I Knew You Were Trouble', writing: '. . . Til you put me down', referring to her song about ex-boyfriend John Mayer: 'Flew to the places I'd never been/'Til you put me down.'

It later emerged that they had indeed split after an 'almighty row' and Taylor left the holiday three days early on 4 January on the first flight she could get back to the US. One newspaper said the split came after Taylor nagged him about his intentions towards other women and that he found her 'too demanding', while another said that Taylor was prioritising her own career commitments over Harry's duties towards 1D and, in the heat of the moment, said that he was 'lucky to be with her'.

How Harry felt about it wasn't known but it seems Richard Branson found out he was staying nearby and invited him to check out Necker. Harry was also said to have had a kite-boarding lesson while he was there and later let off some steam, drinking champagne and eating sushi and jumping in the hot tub.

US reality star Hermione Way was also relaxing in the tub, but when the blonde was questioned by a Directioner on Twitter as to whether anything had happened between them, she denied it. She said: 'I didn't know what had happened. He seemed happy to me. I had a lovely time. Harry is a charming fella.'

Harry certainly had a good time and returned to Gorda in the early hours of the morning, looking somewhat the worse for wear. He was clearly doing his best to put the horrible split behind him. The couple's whirlwind fling had lasted just sixty-five days – and her record label confirmed that she would write a song about their break-up, amid claims she wanted him back.

Many critics and fans were more cynical about the relationship, speculating it was a PR exercise. They commented on the fact that two young popstars with albums to launch and tours to promote would of course gain more publicity from a high-profile romance. Many of their dates took place in very public locations and they didn't seem too worried about being photographed together. Few were surprised therefore when the fling came to an abrupt end.

And the *National Enquirer* said: 'Little does Taylor know that Harry's handlers went to great lengths to put the two together because she's such a huge star.' Their source added:

'Anytime Taylor starts dating a new guy she gets a flurry of media attention, and her breakups receive even more.'

Whatever the true story, Harry's fans rejoiced on Twitter with messages including 'hahaha we all knew this day would be soon', 'let's throw a huge party' and 'praise god, yippee!' Then people started predicting the names of song titles that Taylor might use if she were to write a break-up song about Harry, like she did about her other famous exes. The hashtag #HaylorBreakupSongTitles became a No. 1 trending topic worldwide on Twitter a few hours after news broke of the split.

It wasn't just Directioners delighting in the split. Miley Cyrus made a joke by posting some pictures on Twitter of her and her sister Noah in bed with a life-size cutout of Harry. In one image, both Miley – who was engaged to Liam Hemsworth – and her younger sibling are kissing the cardboard, with Miley writing: 'All I want for my birrfffday is a big booty h**. All @noahcyrus wants for her BIRFFFDAY is @harry_styles.'

Of course this sent Twitter fans into meltdown as they speculated that she had Harry in her sights, so she was forced to write: 'In no way do I want Harry. No offense. I'm sure that'll be a story now 2. I'm happily engaged. Just got saucy with a cardboard cut out.'

After his Necker visit, Harry caught a connecting flight out of Puerto Rico to New York's JFK airport, where he waited three and a half hours before flying into Heathrow. During his stopover he ate at an Italian restaurant, Don

Peppe, with a group of fans, who tucked into shrimp linguini, veal parmesan and baked clams.

Arriving back in London on 6 January, Harry was carrying his guitar case and had an impressive tan. Dressed in a beige jacket, grey t-shirt, blue jeans and his trusty orange beanie, he had an impressive entourage in tow, helping him with his luggage as he walked through Heathrow Terminal 5 after his flight from New York City.

He was back in the UK to help 1D promote 'Kiss You', which dropped on 7 January. Waves of anticipation had been created as music bosses released snapshots of the boys' latest release on their YouTube channel, showing them on skis, motorbikes and in sailors' outfits.

The video's director Vaughan Arnell, who had worked with them on 'Take Me Home' and 'Live While We're Young', told MTV News: 'The ultimate tease, I think it's as you've never seen the boys before, kind of studio-based. I wouldn't say comedy, it's all tongue-in-cheek. I think in the past, the boys have always been outside, it's always been kind of quite location-based, and this is the first studio-based idea I've done with them.'

The video featured loads of green screen work, with lots of references to Elvis Presley's film *Blue Hawaii* and his song 'Jailhouse Rock'. They lark about and are really goofy and Harry even makes a joke regarding his four nipples.

The teasers attracted over 8 million views on YouTube in five days. After the video's release, #KissYouOnVEVO became the top worldwide trending topic on Twitter.

The boys reunited in the New Year at a recording studio in Camden. Harry was seen strolling along the road, and a few unsuspecting girls were delighted when they saw him.

That evening he joined James Corden, Jessie J and Grimmy at a private party hosted by Tinie Tempah, designer Paul Smith and *GQ* magazine editor Dylan Jones at swanky restaurant and club Sketch in Mayfair to celebrate a week of men's London fashion events. He was dressed in a sharp navy suit and was seen leaving the event with pretty brunette actress Alexandra Roach, along with Grimmy and James.

He was obviously putting the pain of the break-up behind him and it was reported that he was planning a boys' holiday to Las Vegas with fellow star Justin Bieber, who had split with his girlfriend Selena.

Across the pond, Taylor was not feeling too sorry for herself either. She was seen visiting a friend with a bottle of red wine, before heading to the People's Choice Awards the following night in Los Angeles. At the event the boys added another two gongs to their stash after winning Favourite Album for *Up All Night* and Favourite Song for 'What Makes You Beautiful'. They weren't there to pick up the awards but instead sent video messages thanking their fans. Meanwhile their arch-rivals The Wanted picked up the Favourite Breakout Artist award, while Taylor scooped the Favourite Country Artist gong.

However, it was not all good news for Taylor: it was reported that ticket sales for her upcoming tour had fallen by a half since the split. Louise Mullock, a spokesperson for ticketing website Seatwave, said: '1D and Taylor Swift are two of the most popular acts in the world and they're consistently among our best-sellers. However, the adulation received by 1D is one of a kind, and the boys' fans are famously protective. Since many of Taylor's fans are also 1D fans, she may have bitten off more than she can chew by dividing their loyalties.'

2012 was a great year for 1D and the boys are hugely excited about their future and what 2013 might bring. For now, they are rehearsing for their tour at every opportunity. They want it to be even bigger and better than their last tour and will give it everything they have.

Harry approaches everything with a light-hearted and fun attitude and it seems his happy-go-lucky ways are contagious. Looking at how far he's come in such a short space of time you could be forgiven for thinking he was far older than he is. The boys have certainly grown up and become more confident as they have taken the world by storm, and they appear to be tighter than ever as a group of friends as well as bandmates.

Harry has said the only thing he would change about his life is to see more of his friends and family who have been with him every step of the way – particularly his mum and Gemma. In five years' time he hopes he will still be on the road with 1D, continuing to break records, meeting new people and playing music.

He confessed: 'I still want to be hanging out with the boys and travelling the world and having hits. I can't imagine anything I'd rather do than this.' Looking back on his journey, Harry says that he can't believe how lucky he is to have had the opportunity and how humbled he is by it.

So what does Harry think is the secret to his phenomenal success? 'I think people see us as down to earth. We don't try to act like big pop stars. We're attainable and we're friendly. None of us have changed and I honestly don't think we will.'